It Won't Rain Because There's Nothing to Stop It

A Madcap Spiritual Journey

A Slightly Revised Edition

Gary Holgate

It Won't Rain Because There's Nothing to Stop It
Slightly Revised Edition
Copyright © 2018 by Gary Holgate

ISBN 978-0-9939570-2-4

Published by Gary Holgate

Cover and Artwork by Gary Holgate

For my brother Ian, the most down-to-earth person I have ever known. Your zest for life was contagious while your smile was infectious. You dealt with responsibility as easily as I shirked it. You embraced family values while I hid from them. You forwent your spirituality in lieu of my practicality, helping me become the person I am today.

Spirituality
[spir-i-choo-uh al-ity] - *adjective*

Traditional definitions pertain to one's spirit or religious beliefs where modern spirituality embraces the inner path or journey and promotes the discovery of one's self through our interaction with all things.

Gary Holgate

Table of Contents

Foreword

I was honoured when asked by Gary to write the forward to this book. I am a Practitioner of Spirit. A poet, psychic, spiritual consultant and cybershaman. I mention this only because I have in my journeys crossed paths with thousands of people who work in the spiritual arts. Those who have had the greatest impact are the ones who were genuine and sincere. Gary is that kind of man.

I have found in the past that most spiritual, self-help, new age books are regurgitated dribble, new age nonsense or the metaphysical meanderings of those who lack true insight or knowledge. The thing that makes this book so refreshing is its simple and straightforward approach. I say 'simple' with respect and admiration. There is a beauty to simplicity; an uplifting truth that transforms and transcends. This tome is a heartwarming journey through one man's spiritual evolution. **If you are looking for answers, this isn't the book for you, for it is less about providing answers and more about inspiring you to look in the mirror and discover the answers within yourself. By sharing stories immersed in good**, we are taken to a place where the divine shines in beautiful ways. Each glimpse into the soul of the writer nurtures our dreams and awakens us to our own truths. This is a significant contribution to both literary and spiritual realms because of its clear and good intention.

Gary has a creativity and passion that illuminates a special purpose meant to serve the highest good. I found myself reliving moments in my own life that encouraged personal transformation. This book is a precious gift that speaks to the heart. In a time of reality TV and tabloid journalism, it is profoundly pleasing to come across something that guides us through the splendors of soul and spirit. Hopefully many who read this will be inspired to experience life in new ways. We are all teachers and healers. With this offering, Gary has taught us compassion and wisdom while infusing the spirit with positive healing energy.

I am pleased and privileged to have been asked to contribute to this enchanting and enriching expression of the self. For me, this book begins and ends with the budgie story. The innocence and purity of this moment in time is a revelation that awakens the heart and opens the soul to light. Its simple genius and ethereal insights liberate the mind that we may see the beauty in our own lives. This book flows with transformational and empowering messages that say simply be exactly who you are.

I say to all sit back, relax, and read yourself into a state of soulful pleasure where every day counts and every moment is an opportunity to create positive change.

Yours in Heartfelt Kindness
MicHEAL Teal

The Ancient One

Preface

Why am I writing a book?

I have been asking myself that very same question. It must be important as I have written this book three times, won the Pulitzer twice, (spelt it correctly once), made the New York Times Best Seller list, even found myself on the *Oprah* show. Of course, this was all in my mind, but that's where it all begins, right?

If I am truly honest, this book was a long time in the making. I was never one to easily commit but this was not from a place of lethargy, more from fear. A great man once lay in bed contemplating life and his many ideas on life, love, and creativity. He was asked why he just lay there thinking about them rather than doing any of the wonderful things he envisioned. He simply said that while he did nothing he had the potential to do or be anything, but upon deciding, he would be limited by his choice. His name was Syd Barret. I am not saying that I am just like Syd, but I do relate to his thought process. I guess I just made a choice.

I always fancied the idea of writing a book, and have talked about it for most of my adult life. Don't get me wrong. I have started a couple but they were fantasy novels and fell victim to my Aries outlook on life and sat unfinished amidst the countless other projects I started. It was not until I offered to help my friend Gordon with his new book that the urge surfaced once again. It was different this time; there seemed to be more focus despite the lack of direction. I was quietly optimistic.

So what could I write about? Using the excuse that chai tea lattes somehow aided my decision- making process, I pondered on the paranormal investigations and workshops I had organized over the years. I really didn't want to write about ghosts or how we collected evidence, after all there are only so many ways to tell the same story. I knew I wanted to include the paranormal on some level and with almost two thousand members spanning three groups, that aspect of my life surely warranted an inclusion.

It was during one particular winter's evening when the relentless snowfall thoughtfully provided me with the opportunity to flex my snow-shoveling muscles that I found myself remembering the story of the budgie when I was six-years-old. As the memories unfolded, a warmth filled me as I recounted that day and unbeknownst to me, uncorked the elixir that was my spiritual journey. It was a "eureka" moment although slightly dampened due to my insistence that I could clear the snow from the driveway wearing my slippers, but I found the direction I had been looking for. I was going to write about the one thing I knew most about, the one subject that required no research or approvals; I was going to talk about myself.

I started with what would become "Just Ask" and as I progressed, more stories came to mind offering additional insights into my own journey. It became apparent that these stories could be used as a voice to help others relate to and identify similar stories within their own journey. The book was born!

So why did I really write this book?

It dawned on me as I thought about my life, in particular the early years, how I demonstrated acts of spirituality without really knowing it. This started with my acknowledgment of a force of energy larger than myself yet still small enough to make a difference in my life. The use of the law of attraction or "Secret" was an interaction with the universe, albeit for juvenile materialistic gain.

I am not ignorant enough to believe that I am alone with these stories. I just don't think we realize or recognize our own spiritual interactions, as they are often lost within the hustle and bustle of our lives. This book covers many topics; some mainstream, others not so much but all relatable. I wanted to demonstrate through my own experiences that you could explore your own adventure just by exploring your own untold stories that comprise your life.

Acknowledgements

Thanks must go to everyone who participated in my life, for these stories would not be possible without you. Special thanks must go to my parents, in particular my father, for apparently I was not the easiest child in the world to live with. I find this very unlikely but people closest to me seem to agree with him and often take his side. I was just very spirited; besides, it's tough growing up when you are always right. Okay, I am starting to see what he meant.

I mentioned my brother in my dedications. He was a large part of my life growing up and it wasn't until I was older did I realize the role he played. We were very much opposites; he was always practical, good with his hands and content with his life. For him, there was never a problem that a good single malt whiskey could not cure. I was a little more complicated which often looked from the outside as lazy or indifferent. I have always been a dreamer drifting through life, always a student and never really compliant to social decorum.

With all of this in mind, I want to thank everyone from my childhood; you all played your part. I would like to name a few now, not for any other reason than they would probably think it was cool that they were mentioned in a book. These are in no particular order and I apologize if I did not mention you; Kirk Payne, Stephen Eddy, Paul Blight, Darren Whippy, Francis Dunne, and David Sutherland. You all know the roles you played; I wish you all happiness and success.

My family; these stories all started with you. In fact, if it weren't for part of our family moving to southern England, I would have never experienced the very first story of this book.

Thanks also go to my Canadian friends and family, past and present. You were there for the beginning of my North American journey and urged me to try new avenues, leading to spiritual paths I may have otherwise overlooked. To Gordon Ellison, who although is a recent friend, has proven to be a true spiritual companion and all round great addition to my life. It was during a psychic fair while helping Gordon that I found not only a new love but a new life.

Indeed, much has changed since this book was first published in 2015. Relationships have moved on and new ones were born. Locations have been many but home is still in my heart. Outside my relationship with Madelyn who is a true being of light, the birth of our daughter Sienna marked the dawn of a new and exciting age.

Introduction

I often find myself day-dreaming about my past. It wasn't until recently that it occurred to me, the spiritual path I strive to follow today is the very same one I followed growing up; I was just not aware of it. Through stories of actual events in my life, my aim is to illustrate how we all follow spiritual paths, and how we might not be aware of them.

As a six-year-old, I reached out to the universe. At eight, I used the law of attraction to follow in the paths of a legendary cowboy. At twelve, my curious observations received direction, while in my adult years; I understood the power a single word can wield.

My life is no different from anyone else's. Perhaps by recounting my own experiences and how they related to my spiritual journey, I can help you discover how your own stories illuminate your own madcap journey.

So what now?

Well, I guess the best place to start would be at the beginning.

When I imagined this book, my reasons were somewhat clouded. I didn't even have any stories past the GPS one and even that was unfinished. It wasn't until I began the writing process that memories and stories invited themselves and the idea was born. I was part way through the budgie story, which later became "Just Ask," when it became very clear to me; I was not just writing about random stories from my life, I was writing about spiritual events that I participated in under the guise of my life.

Just Ask

I was six-years-old when I first realized there was something more out there, something bigger than myself and everyone around me, but still small enough for me to interact with it.

When I was born, the story goes that as I was wrapped in a cloth and handed to my mother; I focused my attention on the nurses and followed their movements around the room. The head nurse turned to my mother.

"Oh, he has been here before," she said.

Okay, nothing major but it does lend itself to some of the theories we will discuss later in the book. Where was I? Oh yes, six years of age.

I have always felt a strong bond to animals, I cannot explain this or why I am affected so much by them, but without sounding callous, in general I feel more for them than I do people. It's not that I don't like or enjoy the company of people, I just think that for the most part we bring things upon ourselves whereas animals are innocent. There are exceptions to the rule as history has illustrated, but in general my empathy is heightened where animals are concerned.

On this particular day, we were heading over to my aunt's house for a party. She was moving to Southern England the following week and the families were getting together to give them a proper send off. Our destination was Rawtenstall, a small sleepy town in Lancashire located in the North West of England. My dad chose to take the scenic route in the hope of avoiding the traffic typically experienced on an early summer Sunday afternoon. To be clear, it was more or less the same as the non-scenic route, only there was more garbage and sheep on the sides of the roads. We headed out of town and began making our way across the moorlands to their house.

About halfway there we came upon an old isolated cotton mill. Long abandoned, this impressive rectangular stone building was as large as a football field. Remarkably, the majority of the top floor windows were still intact, though the lower two floors had succumbed to passing louts, or migratory birds with quite bad eyesight. The reservoir that had once provided life to the mill now offered shelter and sustenance to the local wildlife as nature slowly reclaimed the land.

Having grown tired of the customary "are we there yet?" game from the safety of the back seat; I turned my attention to the scenery as it passed by in a blur. It was at that time I turned to look out of the front window. I am not really sure what caused me to look but at that second I saw a budgie fly across the front of the car and land in the field behind the mill. A period of calm followed where I politely asked my dad to pull the car over and afford me the opportunity to locate the said bird.

Okay, it didn't go down quite like that. Using the car seat in front of me to provide leverage, I pulled myself up while screaming at my dad to stop the car. After what seemed like an eternity, this approach resulted in a plethora of curses from my dad, a promise that I would be soon sporting his foot from a rather delicate orifice, and that the bird was getting further away. It was then that I started kicking the back of my dads seat. Though the cramped space prevented much in the way of leverage, my enthusiasm more than made up for this.

Sensing that my approach had finally paid dividends, I returned to my seated position as my dad gently brought the car to a halt on the side of the road.

Again, this is not how it really went down. Having cursed in a language I am pretty sure he invented on the spot, he handled the Vauxhall in a fashion that would have made Steve McQueen proud. Akin to a scene from *Bullit,* loose gravel exploded from the wheels as we came to an abrupt stop on the hard shoulder, sending sheep and roadside litter scattering.

Now, let's all agree that a few brief moments of calm discussion transpired before I was given a short time to find the bird.

I walked towards the dry-stone wall that surrounded the field as both excitement and fear rose within me.

What if I couldn't find the bird?

Would it be okay?

Would my dad's shoe really fit there?

All good questions, but my mind snapped back to the present as I reached the wall. I gingerly climbed. The calm discussion that transpired in the car had left a lasting impression on my backside, causing me to wince slightly as I sat atop of the wall. Staring out at the field, I quickly realized that it was far bigger than it had looked from the car.

Where was I going to start? The grass was tall, as tall as my waist; and the typical hardy grass found in the moorlands surrounding our town. Though the grass was dense, it offered relief in small clearings where wild flowers and thistles had taken root, encouraging passing bees to take an inquisitive respite.

It was a sunny day, not too hot but one of those days where you can wear just a pair of shorts and a vest and feel comfortable. I proceeded carefully. My eyes scanned the dense vegetation for any signs of life as I made way into the field. All I could think about was how alone and scared that bird must be. *How would I feel if I was lost like that?* I was determined to find it.

Time passed. My mind wandered for brief periods as I caught glimpses of Red Admiral butterflies and felt the furry flowers that crowned the grass tickle my legs. At one point, I stopped and slowly turned around in a circle, hoping to catch a glimpse of the bird. My dad, who had demonstrated saint-like patience through this ordeal, called to me and indicated that we should get going.

I have to say, I am not religious, was not raised with religion, and have never read the bible or any other theological scripture. With that in mind, I am not sure why I did what I did next. I stopped turning in the field and faced my dad. He was around two-hundred feet from me, leaning over the wall. I looked up and can still vividly remember the words I spoke.

"If there is anyone or anything up there, I know you don't want the bird to die."

At that second, it was literally the second I stopped speaking, the bird flew from around mid-way between my dad and myself and landed a few feet from me. I picked up the bird and headed back to the car. I held the bird on the back seat until I got to my aunt's where we got a box for him. I had that budgie for another seven years before he passed.

So what did I learn from this?

Well, for me it was a light bulb moment, despite my tender age. From that point on I knew that there was something else out there. Even though I couldn't see it, I knew it was always there to call upon. It was almost like the force from Star Wars, an analogy pointed out to me when I was to visit Lily Dale in the U.S. many years later. As a child, I was not conflicted by what society might think about what had just happened. I was innocent, and accepted things as a person who has no reason to judge or to question what they see or believe. As we grow, life gets in the way. We are taught how to think, how to question, and how to ignore. I was lucky that my moment came when I was open and innocent enough to accept it for what it was.

Does this mean you have missed your moment?

Of course not. We are all looking for our own moment in the field. We focus so hard on the moment that we often miss everything else in the field. Stop to notice the butterflies, the bees, even the way the grass feels on your legs, and how they all play their parts. It's the sum of what is around you at all times, not one defining element. Once you are *accepting* without doubt and *knowing* instead of wishing or hoping, you are ready for your moment. At that time you won't need to find your field, it will find you.

As a child I *accepted* and *believed* what I experienced was real, real to me. I just assumed everyone knew about it. I had not been taught to the contrary so asking for help to save the bird was something I didn't doubt, question or really give much thought to; I just asked.

As we grow older, we lose the ability to accept without question. We tend to fall into the rhythms of our family and social circles as we conform to the life expected of us. We always have the choice and opportunities to see life as we did when we were without doubt in our acceptance; it is just sometimes difficult to shake off the trappings of life and just ask.

Root Chakra
Muladhara

PHYSICAL NEEDS

Muladhara is symbolized by a lotus with four petals and the colour red.

Streamline

G rowing up in a single parent home was not that bad. I never wanted for anything, save more time with Dad, and it did offer lots of free time for myself, which I always welcomed. After the budgie incident, I often found myself preoccupied on all manner of things; things a six-year-old probably should not have been dwelling on. Don't get me wrong; I still acted very childlike, as I do today, but there was more. I always had a feeling that I knew something but it constantly eluded me, staying just out of reach. To be honest it was quite frustrating. It was almost like trying to remember "that actor" in "that movie" when you pass thirty and have a mind full of senseless worry. Or experiencing that moment when you lose a simple word at the worst possible time, reducing you to a game of charades because for some reason the word "climb" has been completely removed from your vocabulary.

Now, as much as I dwelled, I daydreamed. I daydreamed a lot. It was during this period that I discovered what we know today as "The Secret."

I was around seven or eight when I first called upon the Law of Attraction.

Clint Eastwood was a childhood hero of mine. The man with no name, the thousand-yard-stare and the endless supply of half-chewed cigars; he had it all as far as cowboys go. Groups of us often pooled our meager funds together to buy caps for our toy guns; we would then head out into the nearby woods for an often-contested shoot-out. I brandished a rather hefty Colt replica most of the time, but the gun I really wanted was the Streamline.

I don't actually recall Clint using that type of gun but the marketing geniuses used an image of him holding it on the box, sporting his steely stare, and that was good enough for me. It was during one of these spells of daydreaming when I changed my focus from wishing I had the gun to picturing myself actually playing with the gun. It was not a conscious change as far as I recall. It was similar to that moment when you are able to ride your bicycle unassisted for the first time. You never really know what changed or what you did differently; you are just able to do it.

With a recently acquired birch twig for a cigar and my best attempt at a sunbaked squint, I swept through our shoot-outs with the ease that only a seasoned gun fighter possessed. With my imaginary steed beneath me, we clipitty-clopped our way to legendary status. Again, this was all in my mind, but I am blessed with the ability to generate emotions and vivid perceptions of reality, which really helps.

It could have been weeks or months, it is hard to remember that far back, but I do remember the day my dad bought me Streamline. I didn't even ask for it, but on the morning of my brother's birthday, Streamline and I made eye contact for the first time.

Running from my upstairs bedroom, I launched myself from a record-breaking tenth step, landing awkwardly at the bottom of the stairs. I stayed crouched behind the hanging coats and silently listened for my dad's approaching footsteps. Despite the new record, I was sure he would not share my enthusiasm given we had repeatedly damaged the joists holding up the floor due to our inability to listen to reason. Satisfied that he had not heard me or had better things to do, I reached for the bannister, I swung myself up and through the door and into the dining room.

Silence struck, which was strange given the fact I had just stood on the dog. What was that I spied across the room? Could it really be the object of my obsession? I approached with caution, my gun fighter senses heightened. My hands tingled as I mimicked the finger wriggle Clint exercised before every gunfight. I reached the mantle above the fireplace. Streamline had the advantage of higher ground, but I was ready. I held my breath in order to steady my stance, my left hand still wriggling causing a distraction as my right hand poised, almost there... *slap*. Streamline's victory echoed with the familiar sound of my dad's hand cuffing the back of my head.

"Not until Ian opens his presents," my dad said as he continued past me into the kitchen.

It was my brother's birthday, but to stop me from pouting for the following two months because he got presents and I didn't, I also got one. I know, it was technically HIS birthday, but at some point the decision had been made to buy each of us one present on the other's birthday. You had to hand it to Lady Democracy, for on that particular day, she had delivered me Streamline.

We ruled the Wild West which was the old bomb shelter that lined the back streets of our neighborhood. It was not until one fateful day when I thought it would be funny to wake my dad by shooting the gun next to his ear, that we parted ways. I blame the cap manufacturers. How was I supposed to know that there was a tendency for the caps to flare on occasion?

Well, this was that occasion and my dad's hair bore the scars of a living room shoot-out. Accompanied by the acrid scent of burning human hair and that all too familiar sting on my backside, I began what seemed like a life sentence of bedroom incarceration while Streamline found a new home.

What did I learn from all this?

Well, without stating the obvious, don't shoot your dad, even if it is just with a cap gun. Even at this early age, I was starting to realize more and more that focusing on things really seemed to help make them a reality. Not just thinking or wishing for them as that reinforced the idea that I didn't have them, but by using my imagination to really visualize a reality where I already had them.

The ability to "put your self there" is key to visualization. Not everyone can do it to a beneficial level, and some need help attaining that emotional connection through focus.

For some reason whenever I manage to achieve something, be it law of attraction, lucid dreaming or even astral projection, it normally takes two weeks for me to attain my goals. Once I have succeeded, I seem to lose the desire to try it again. I often wonder why I don't ask for more. I have quite the vivid imagination so I would have no problems coming up with a wish list, but it's as though once I prove it to myself I then move on. Perhaps I should have envisioned a life where I had two Streamline guns. Maybe next time.

Reach for the Stars

There have been three occasions where I used the Law of Attraction. The first time I stumbled upon it at the age of eight, the third and last time I was thirty and I will talk about that last one later in the book.

I was twelve years of age when I called upon the universe to deliver the object of my desire for the second time. I was entering my teenage years, had a mind full of questions, and I was obsessed with astronomy.

Living in a row of terraced houses, similar to the ones you see on Coronation Street and many industrialized areas in the north of England, my solar field of vision consisted of a twenty-foot radius above my back yard. Nestled between two rather large overgrown weeds, a mass of telephone cables and some rather large braziers on my neighbor's washing line, earth's orbiting natural satellite was not the only moon I often observed.

Our backyards were not your customary oasis of lawn and flowers you typically see in North America. They were more a throwback to the Second World War and often as dreary. For many years and even to this day, each backyard consisted of a concrete square no larger than a small living room and came equipped with a bomb shelter.

Ours had long since been converted into an outhouse and storage shed, but our neighbors had their bomb shelter until the early nineties. The back street dividing the houses had a long drain running the length with cast iron grates at regular intervals. Some people still heated their homes with coal fires so there was often a rusting cast iron coal door in the backyard walls allowing for the coalmen to make their weekly delivery. I still remember the horse drawn carts of the coal and rag and bone men as they navigated our tight reinforced concrete back street playground while we followed closely behind, attempting to hitch a ride on the back of the old wooden wagons.

In the midst of all this, I discovered the small clear patch of sky that was my gateway to a world of imagination and escape. I started with my dad's binoculars, though they didn't offer much more of a vantage over my naked eye. I tended to find myself staring into the windows of the house that owned the large brazier more than anything as I figured I had a greater chance to glimpse an earthbound wonder than the sea of tranquility.

The object of my desire was a refractor telescope. It was not a huge telescope, but it was a great leap from the binoculars, and it offered the potential to view more than the mammary galaxies of the lady across the back street, not that I was complaining.

A rather seedy secondhand store that I passed each day had the telescope I wanted. As the centerpiece to a clumsily organized window display sporting an old wedding dress stained in all the wrong places, a tarnished silver tea set once used to store dentures, and five well-read issues of Playboy from the seventies, the telescope was displayed with pride.

In retrospect, perhaps I should have been looking elsewhere, but there is an innocence of youth that has the ability to see only what it wants to see. This trait often led to many a heated discussion with my dad regarding the correct method to clean the dishes.

Being a little older than the last time I had wanted anything as bad as Streamline, I was more prepared. With Streamline, I achieved my goal without the awareness of how my thoughts and feelings could help manifest themselves in the real world.

This time, it was going to be different. I set myself a regiment of thoughts, feelings, and beliefs that spanned the full day. Upon waking, I imagined myself having to step around the telescope as it stood proud, clad with last night's socks in the middle of my bedroom.

During school, I doodled on my exercise books portraying the previous night's journey through the cosmos. Eating supper, I watched the night sky darken ever so slowly as I eagerly waited for my date with the stars. I still used the binoculars at night but I imagined them being the telescope. I would close one eye and peer through them, imagining that the now single lens looked beyond what I could see, and far back into history.

This went on for two weeks before I began to lose interest. Nothing had happened and I had put so much energy into it. I had dropped hints along the way, though I knew we did not have the money to buy "such a lavish toy," as my dad had put it.

"Can you get my tool box from the car, Gary?"

It was a Monday night, and we were decorating the bedroom that I shared with my brother. I am not sure what importance the day of the week adds, but hey, I actually remembered it so I wanted to include it. My dad's voice still hung in my ears as I walked slowly from the bedroom, covered in pieces of damp wallpaper and globules of paste.

"Can Ian not go?" I asked in the most pathetic voice I could muster given I had just decided to see what wallpaper paste tasted like.

"No, you go," he insisted.

I left the bedroom to my brother laughing silently at me but making no effort to conceal the fact that he was actually silently laughing at me.

What I pictured happening to him is unimportant, but yet again, the universe let me down.

Opening the boot, or trunk for our North American readers, I caught a glimpse of a white box. It was a large box filling the boot, leaving no space for my dad's tools. I grabbed the box and lifted it partially out of the car. It was quite heavy but nothing I couldn't manage. Resting the box on the edge of the boot, I rotated it so that I could see the label on the bottom of the box. It read "60mm Refractor Telescope." The rest of that night escapes me, but I would assume I helped my dad finish the wallpapering without grumbling.

I cannot remember the actual brand, maybe it was a Tasco, but I do remember it was radiant white with a wooden stand, an accessories tray, and a small side focuser. I shared many a wondrous year with my telescope. On occasion we even loaded it up into the car and headed out to the nearby moorlands where the full vista offered unlimited possibilities. I still looked in on big brazier from time to time, though I found it a little more difficult to focus given the short distance. I kept the binoculars handy.

So what did I learn this time?

I was not prepared for how long I had to maintain the intention. I don't think there is a set time as it's not really an exact science, but with me it seems to take two weeks to achieve my goals. If and when you decide to give this a try, don't expect to think of something and have it delivered to your door the next day. I am not saying that this cannot happen, but use your common sense here. You increase the possibility that your intention could come to fruition by ensuring there are feasible avenues of delivery.

What do I mean by this?

Let's say for argument's sake that you ask for a million dollars. If your available circle includes a wealth of personal bankers or affluent people with funds available, then your odds could increase dramatically. It could still be delivered without any of those factors in your favor. It may take more time and effort due to the limited avenues you have to receive the funds. There are no rules here; you need to forget about the values we place on things, it's all the same to the universe.

So, to sum it all up, here is what I took from this latest interaction with the universe. Don't eat wallpaper paste; it's not as good as you might first think and this Law of Attraction thing really seems to work.

Above all else, the one thing I really took from all this was that my dad had lied; there were no tools.

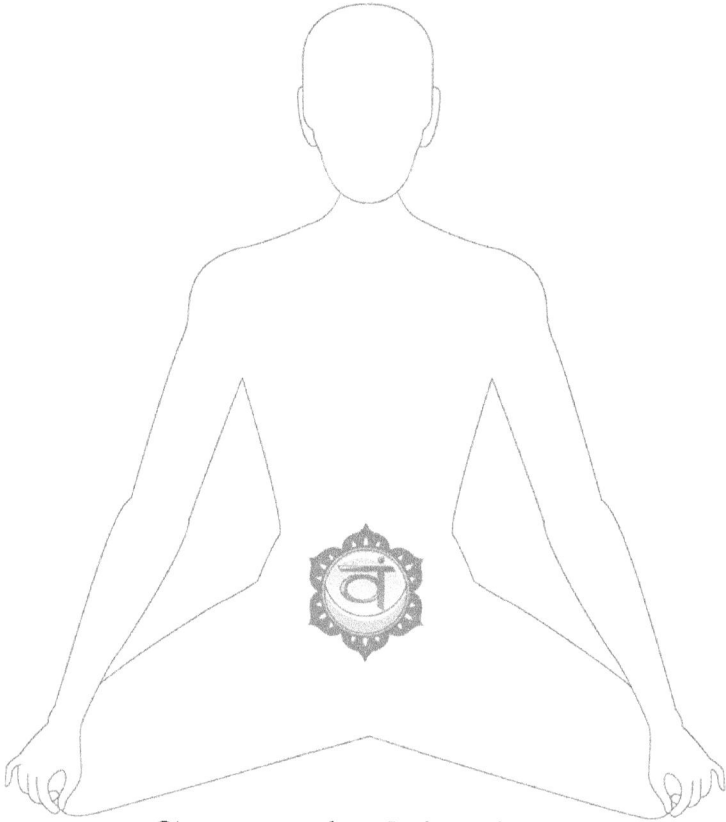

Sacral Chakra
Swadhisthana

SEXUALITY, EMOTIONS

Swadhisthana is symbolized by a white lotus within which is a crescent moon with six vermilion or orange petals.

In The Flames

I have always had a fascination with candles and more specifically, with flames. It is mesmerizing to sit and watch the way they move and react to energy; it is as though they have a life of their own.

I began my journey into magic at quite an early age. Nobody in my family practiced, or at least, not to my knowledge, but I was continually drawn to it like a moth to a flame. Growing up as I did in the middle of witch country must have been more than a coincidence. I was later to discover that Holgates had even been involved in the witch trials of 1632, but this had no influence on me as a ten-year-old.

I was no stranger to witches and rituals as I lived a short walk from an old castle in a good-sized woods that saw its fair share of activities. The building dated back almost a thousand years and was shrouded by legends of ghosts, monsters, secret passages, and of course, witchcraft. At around eight years of age I remember often being in the woods late at night with a bunch of my friends as we bet each other to see who could get closest to the witches as they performed their rituals. In the moorlands, a short walk from the woods, make-shift altars were not uncommon as ritualistic animal sacrifice occasionally found its home within the headlines of the local tabloids. It was a different time for sure.

I am not sure how I came to own my first book on magic, but I recall reading it cover to cover many times before decided to take the plunge. It was a book on candle magic, and if I am to be really honest, I wanted it mainly to get a girlfriend. Being a wide-eyed eleven-year-old boy, details were never really that important to me, which led to me skimming through most of the book to the "good bits." In retrospect, the section regarding spell work returning three-fold springs to mind as a somewhat important omission caused by my impatience and youthful ignorance.

Fortunately for me, the three-fold return was never really an issue, not that I had noticed anyway. For all I know, it had returned and I simply ignored it, did not notice it or I just sucked at all this magic and three-fold of no effect is, well, no effect.

I quickly discarded the book in favor of developing my own spells. It felt more natural and I could make up rhymes that had girls' names in them. I created a small altar for myself in an area in my bedroom. This consisted of a few large books, an Action Man figure box, and a stack of records that had no right being in anyone's collection. In retrospect, keeping the box from my Action Man might have been a wiser option, given the climate for retro toys, but at the time, it was the perfect height to hold my candles.

It did not take long for word to spread to my friends that I was doing magic with candles; this was helped in part by me telling everyone that I was doing magic with candles. Some friends thought it was weird, others thought it was cool and some just had no opinion at all, or were afraid I would turn them into a frog or something and thought it best to just smile and keep quiet.

I performed many spells during those early years and also developed my curiosity for ESP phenomena, energy, and psychic vampires before I had turned thirteen.

By the time I was sixteen, I had amassed quite a collection of books ranging from advanced candle magic, druid and pagan arts, psychic development and one book on black magic. It was the latter that occupied my thoughts more than any of the others. I am not sure if it was the influence of heavy metal music from a very early age or just a teenage rebellion, but there it was. I remember visiting a bookstore in Howarth, which is well known for its witchcraft, where I asked for the book *Dark Side of The Moon* by Basil E. Crouch. I had heard it was a balanced mix of dark and light magic with an absence of any sort of bias. The store owner looked at me with a blank stare before blurting, "We don't have that here," and vanished through a curtain into the back of the store. That just made me want it even more.

I was fascinated with the subject of the occult and higher magic within those circles. It was not necessarily evil though the reputation it portrayed painted a far more ominous picture, but it was different and very taboo. I even went as far as seeking out a girlfriend who was a Satanist. Though looking back, I think she just had smoked too much of the old green leaf and listened to way too many Black Sabbath albums. She was most certainly not a Satanist as I understood them in my later years.

As I researched further, I noticed stories in the newspapers relating to this very subject. It could have been a coincidence or perhaps they were always present and I had simply not previously noticed them, but stories of covens in the woods and animal sacrifice on make-shift altars suddenly seemed to dominate the news. I didn't seek out a coven, though I did visit the local spiritual churches more frequently for guidance and a sense of belonging.

It was during this time that I discovered our family name played a prominent role in the witch trials of 1632. Tracing back our line, there was a split in names that we could not explain. Perhaps an illegitimate child or as we suspected, involvement in the proceedings caused a relocation of the family and possibly a name change. It was difficult to tie our current family to the Holgates of the seventeenth century given the lack of records, but it could answer a lot of questions. Being classed a witch five hundred years ago could be the result of saying a simple curse during an argument, to an herbalist using nature's ingredients to relieve ailments. Invariably, during those dark times, it meant death if you were accused and found guilty.

Today, you can study the very same concepts and receive a degree and respected career; what a difference a few hundred years can make.

So what does magic mean to me?

I never really gave it much thought until a few years ago. I was so wrapped up in the "How To" that I put no thought into the "Should I?" There was no spell or ritual that was off limits to me, though following Crowley into the realms of the Abramelin was not something I was about to do.

As I started to really think about what magic meant to me, I thought more of the actual rituals and the ceremonies. They are designed to elicit a state of mind and energy that breathe life and emotion into an intention. The more I meditated and the more I thought about the ceremonies, it dawned on me that I didn't really need them. A bold statement indeed, but we are capable of so much. Many of the rituals we use every day have been passed down for many years. They are altered as they pass through hands, but the underlying fundamentals remain. The same spell can be found many times, but yet they seem to point towards the same purpose.

Where did spells originate?

Personally I think that for the most part, they were stumbled upon. You have to put yourself in Medieval Britain six hundred years ago. It was a far more simple time where things were accepted at face value and due to the inability to travel or explore, people were easily influenced. Over time, individuals who lived around nature often found that certain plants helped to cure or relieve ailments. This could have been as simple as rubbing a dock leaf on nettle stings to remove the irritation.

As children we all knew this, it was one of those old wives' tales passed down through generations to become common knowledge. It's hard to imagine that as recently as a few hundred years ago, offering this simple act could be construed as the devil's work and lead to you being branded a witch.

Luckily we are an inquisitive bunch and 'stuck it to the man' albeit the medieval man, leading to individuals who started to wonder that if nature provided one cure then it stood to reason that it could also provide cures for others, and thus the birth of herbalism.

So how did these acts turn into spells and rituals that we know today?

Well, like with most things, using the herbal approach to medicine is never one hundred percent effective as there are simply far too many variables that could affect the outcome. With superstition being more common than swamp foot in those days, if one particular approach was found to produce results, it was often copied. Let's follow this through from a simple discovery to a spell we may use today.

We will use the nettle and dock leaf for this example.

Picture a small rural setting where farming was the dominant livelihood. With this in mind it would stand to reason that the common-folk would be out in the fields during the early hours before dawn. The diminished light often made it difficult to avoid coming into contact with unseen nettles in the field that in turn could see these folks pay a visit to the local herbalists for treatment. Through trial and error, the herbalists found that pummeling many leaves into a paste and applying it as a salve produced better results than a single leaf applied in the field.

As this pattern repeated itself and evolved through word of mouth, it would soon become common knowledge to perform the dock leaf spell before the morning sun rose on any day but a Sabbath using a dock leaf paste application. Many variations would surface as other herbalists would change the spell based on their own circumstances and available plant life. Perhaps these remedies were not always from a place of knowing, but more through trial, error, luck, coincidence, and just maybe copious amounts of their preferred fermented beverage.

People in medieval England and for much of Europe were very fickle, easily led, and succumbed to tales relayed by passing travellers. It is easy to see how many of the spells and rituals commanded such power and belief through such tales.

Before all the witches out there stand up at once in protest, remember the rule of three, and afford me the opportunity to explain.

I am not saying that all the spells are not worth the paper they are written on, but I do believe it is the intent behind the words and not the words themselves that provides the power. As spells are passed down, they take on a role and carry an expectation of success, and why not?

For hundreds of years covens and solitary witches have used the same spells to great success. The more they are used, the more they are trusted and the more chance of success they potentially have. Not because the words get more powerful or are more relevant in our time, but because we believe in them more. If they have worked for all those witches then they must work for us too. It's the power the spell and a ritual command that helps you not only breathe life into the visualization but create an emotional response and belief that the spell will indeed work. By performing the spell, it is almost as if you share a bond with all the witches before you. What if you could capture that exact same elevation of emotion and belief in a moment's thought? Would you still need the ritual?

More recently, I have been trying to achieve that very same level of energy and emotion by meditation or by simply adjusting my own psyche to produce the same results. I believe that like any muscle, through practice we have everything we need inside ourselves to reach our goals. I am not saying that I am going to tear down my altar or discard my herbs, oils, and crystals, but I will continue to try to reduce my dependency on them.

When did I start thinking about this approach?

It was during a meditation.

A common practice when meditating is to create a protective shell around us to deflect negative energy and keep the white light close to us. This can be incorporated into an existing meditation or performed specifically to obtain this desired protection. As you practice this meditation, you can reduce the time it takes to produce this protective effect to just a few seconds. The amount of energy and emotion felt within the short visualization can be as powerful as the energy felt during an hour-long meditation, so why can't we use this approach for all our spiritual and light work?

I have also attempted this approach to reduce my chakra balancing meditation from twenty-six minutes to around twenty seconds. I achieved this by removing the need to visualize every movement of the white light down to the fundamentals of the meditation, which is to balance my chakras. This is particularly useful for those times where you find yourself falling prey to your surroundings, leading to a negative emotional response.

So what did I do to reduce this approach back to its fundamental origins?

I imagined a white light from the source merging with each chakra causing them to burst like individual super novae within my body. This happens almost like a chain reaction, with the effect from one triggering the same effect in the next. This provides energy and balance to my chakras allowing me to focus this energy into a small direct point generating an emotional and physical response. It does take some time to perform this meditation and even after months of practice, I cannot achieve the effect every time, but when I can, it is almost like a rapid moving wave of energy rising up though my body, leaving my chakras balanced.

To help you achieve this, think of the times when you are suddenly scared, or the first kiss of a new relationship. That burst of emotion is very powerful and by recalling that time and putting yourself in that moment, you can recall how you felt at the time.

Using the chakra balancing meditation as the example, as you perform your regular meditation, pick your favorite chakra and make note of how you feel the moment that chakra is balanced. Feel the release of emotion and energy that extends out from your body, saturating the surrounding area as it merges with the light. Remember how you feel at that precise moment; remember the emotion it generates and how it affects your mind and physical body.

Later that day, try balancing that single chakra by recalling the emotion and feeling from the meditation. Allow the emotion to spark the chakra into life, generating the surge of energy accompanying the balancing of the chakra.

If you can harness this at will, then your possibilities are limited only by your own thoughts and emotions.

So what did I learn from this?

My affinity towards candle magic has not really waned and continues to play a prominent role in my life. Having recently completed my Reiki Levels One and Two, I am now looking for ways to include magic into my reiki sessions as a way to incorporate that intuitive part of my life. One of the biggest lessons for me as I look back on my journey and in particularly, the role of magic, is that I should trust my own ability to make a difference from within without having to rely on external influences or tools. I am not going to go and discard all that I have been accustomed to using over the years, but I will be looking for ways reduce my reliance on them and look for ways to use my new approach of Think, Feel, Believe.

I must stress that I do perform spells using the methods I have developed over the years and follow the doctrine when it suits my requirements. There is almost a feeling of comfort within them that promotes calmness within my psyche. This new approach is a work-in-progress and though I doubt it would ever replace my more traditional methods, it adds variation and opportunities when practicality dictates.

It Won't Rain Because There's NothingTo Stop It

Yes, that is exactly what I thought the first time I heard these pearls of wisdom. In order to put this into some perspective, I need to go back to my spritely youth.

I was sixteen, had just completed high school, and thought I knew everything. My college route was all mapped out but I had some lingering doubts regarding my choices. My friends were heading off into their various careers; it was a confusing time for sure.

With my college course not starting for almost five months, and the fact I had no money for our weekends on the beer, I decided that I would give Youth Training a chance.

What is Youth Training? A government-assisted program offering youths a chance to learn a trade over a three-year period.

I chose joinery.

The day came and I arrived at the local business where I would serve my time. As it happened, my exploits as a joiner would only last for a brief three-month period, but at the time I thought I was embarking on a three-year adventure into wood chips and varnish. So there I stood with two other training hopefuls, our vacant demeanor only surpassed by our sheer lack of basic woodworking skills. It was at this time that we were told we would be paired up with a real-life full-fledged joiner. I was getting nervous. What happened if I got paired up with someone I didn't like, or worse, who didn't like me?

I would spend my days making tea, cleaning, and generally doing all the jobs nobody else wanted to do. It was like being back in the schoolyard waiting to be picked for a game of football. Or that time we played Spin-the-Bottle in the old changing rooms, knowing the last person picked would end up with Donkey Kong. Please, pick me first.

I was picked last.

Why was I picked last?

I was bigger than the other two, sported an enthusiastic grin, and had presented myself well above my station. The latter being quite an achievement given the fact I was going through my Woodstock phase. The only conclusion I could draw was that maybe a joiner typically did not turn up for work wearing a tie-died headband, a baggy pink Floyd t-shirt and open-toed sandals. There could have also been a slight chance that I emitted an essence of transcendence, commonly known as hashish. If all this wasn't enough, I now had drool forming in the corners of my mouth due to the unnatural grin I sported; I'm starting to see why I was picked last.

It didn't take me long to realize that we were not the only ones bound to the schoolyard method of selection; the joiners also had a pecking order, and I was paired up with Donkey Kong. His name wasn't really Donkey or even Kong, but for the life in me, I cannot recall his real name, so let's refer to him as Trevor.

Trevor...he was a character. He had a hunched back, a belly sporting years of neglect, social assistance eye glasses bent to allow him to peer above them, and a limp caused by both a pigeon AND duck foot. I really didn't know if I should shake his hand, give him a hug or run for the hills. I went with the handshake. If that had been everything, it was already more than a highly imaginative teen with a propensity for practical jokes could manage, but as I was to find out later that day, there was more.

Trevor could not look up or down. I swear it's true. There was some complication with the hump that prevented his neck from titling vertically. Now joiners find themselves having to look up and down quite frequently, I know this because the *Youth Training Handbook for Budding Joiners* states:

"We are excited you chose this progressive program. The duration of the course will not exceed three years during which time you will be required to look up and down quite frequently; we just thought you should know."

We finished our introductions and the brief yet informative speech on how we are number one in bathrooms and kitchens, and off we all trotted. The day was moving along nicely as I pondered my recent career choices, given that I was in a van with no working seat belts, and for some reason could not shake those life-shattering moments I shared with Donkey Kong that fateful evening.

With lingering goose bumps and a sudden onset of dry mouth, we pulled up to our last job of the day. A second floor bathroom window awaited our professional attention, and I was really not prepared for what happened next.

With his right foot planted, providing support through his extended duck foot, Trevor began to lean backwards. As the weight of the hump tipped his balance, the left leg rose, allowing the pigeon toe to gently brush the ground producing a perfect pointe. With momentum on his side, Trevor forced his neck into his back creating as much of a curve as he could muster given his physical limitations. It was at this time that he started to gently wheeze while his face turned a healthy rose. I almost lost it. As I struggled to maintain my composure and wondered if this would be on the joinery exam, he stuck out his tongue.

I actually think I peed a little; there was a definite presence of moisture, as the customer's bemused look offered no composing help. Even at sixteen I understood the importance of tact, but this was pushing my juvenile capacity of understanding and acceptance to the limit.

How was this not part of the handbook? At the very least it warranted an inclusion as a sealed supplement titled "Open in the Event that Trevor Looks Up."

Despite the obvious distractions, we made a good team. Trevor turned out to be quite the teacher and was never short of wood-related wisdoms. On one particular Friday afternoon, we were heading back to the shop having just completed a job at a local car showroom. Despite spending a full day watching Trevor look up at me as we replaced a second floor showroom window, I felt down.

"What's up?" Trevor asked as he navigated the afternoon traffic like only he could.

"I am supposed to be going to an outdoor concert this weekend, but it looks like it is going to rain," I replied with a downtrodden, the-world-is-over tone that only a teenager could legally pull off.

With a strange sort of huffed wheeze that I can only presume was a chuckle, Trevor croaked, "No, you will be fine. It won't rain because there's nothing to stop it."

Not typically short of words, a trait that followed me into adulthood, I sat in silence. The radio played the current top ten hits and loose tools in the back of the van rattled as Trevor weaved his way through the traffic.

"What?" I finally broke my silence.

"What, what?" Trevor responded with a genuine look of confusion.

"What is that supposed to mean?" I asked.

"It won't rain because there's nothing to stop it," Trevor repeated.

"I heard you the first time. What does that even mean?"

He just smiled, cracked a Kit Kat, offered me a piece and continued through the traffic with frightening determination.

I left shortly afterwards to follow my career into the hi-tech world of business and computers so we never spoke of it again. Over the following years, I forgot about that dull Friday afternoon drive but those indelible words always stuck with me.

So, what does all this have to do with my spiritual journey?

Absolutely nothing, but why should I be the only one who has to carry that vision into perpetuity?

All jokes aside, it really didn't dawn on me why it was important until I started writing this book. I have been throwing this phrase out like it was a line from *Pulp Fiction* with no real thought as to what it meant to myself or more importantly, to anyone else. Then it dawned on me; it's not the phrase that is important but what the phrase represents.

Seriously, what does all this have to do with my spiritual journey?

It's simple. Our interactions with other people, no matter how small, can have more of a lasting impression than we can know. This was a harmless line passed on to me in a shared Kit Kat moment, but I think back to the readings I have done, and the advice given, and I am left to wonder if I ever took liberties with the information.

Did I elaborate on my interpretation of the information I received?

We all have a responsibility to ensure we communicate from a place of knowing, a place of innocence and a place of humble truth. I am not saying that you should not chat or shoot the proverbial poo-bah. Just be aware that no matter how innocent your words may seem at the time, they could have a last impression and not always for the right reasons.

As you embark or continue along your spiritual path, remember this is a great responsibility you have undertaken. Have faith in yourself, have faith in others, and above all remember, it won't rain because there's nothing to stop it.

Solar Plexus Chakra
Manipura

POWER, VITALITY

Manipura is symbolized by a downward pointing triangle with ten
petals, along with the colour yellow.

Purple Parrot

During my teen years I survived many changes within my home life, social circles and within myself. I was still dabbling with magic, the occult, and just about everything 'beyond-normal.' Amidst all this teenage exploration, I stumbled across astral projection and lucid dreams.

Now, in my mature years I developed the skill and patience to disseminate information and make rational decisions and judgments. As a teenager, if it was in a book then it was good enough for me. Reading one particular book on astral projection and lucid dreams, it suggested that in order to embark on this new journey, I needed to expand my mind.

As an adult with some years under my belt, this referred to breaking free of my physical trappings, opening my mind to new spiritual possibilities and to lend and build upon my current knowledge and experiences. As a teenager this meant one thing; I needed to get high.

Being a hippy for the majority of my life, putting my hands on some of the leafy green stuff was not a problem. Masking the smell from my dad required a little more ingenuity. If you are familiar with the scene from *Apollo 13* where they have to figure out how to fit the square filters into a round hole, you would truly appreciate the apparatus I erected in my bedroom. Under the guise that it was an energy collector, I added a green and red spotlight for effect. The idea being that to discharge negative energy I would sit under the red light while the green light drew positivity from the coiled tube that I fed through the window. Luckily for me, I was already playing out of left field enough that my dad had given up trying to figure me out, and generally accepted me for the "weirdo" that I was.

It didn't take long for me to realize there were inherit problems with this method. Within a few minutes of smoking, I found myself day-dreaming about the possibility of life within a Pink Floyd album cover and more importantly, I had forgotten what it was that I was trying to accomplish. Not wanting to be labeled a quitter, I threw myself into my research, feet first into the breach dear friends. Many months later, a dozen or so IOUs that my dad now held over my immediate future, and seven pounds more of me to love due to Mr. Munchy, it dawned on me that I should possibly look for an alternative approach.

I sat beneath my green light of positivity pondering my next move. Despite it being days since I last participated in a solitary weed circle, I was half convinced this green light thing actually worked. It was that or I was now permanently baked. Either way, I felt at peace. My mind wandered to the possibility that smoking the ganja could actually cause lasting mental damage but this was quickly dismissed, as the walking hammers on my Pink Floyd poster started moving. Perhaps this change was coming at the right time after all.

I needed something that would allow me to let loose my spiritual wings while maintaining initial focus and did not require me to go two rounds with a strawberry tart. Along came "Pink Panther."

You will be forgiven in thinking that I spent many nights plopped in front of the TV watching cartoon re-runs. This is not to say that I didn't see the Pink Panther, or even talked to him on occasion, just not in the way you were innocently thinking. Ahhhhhh, the penny drops.

So down the rabbit hole I went. The initial goal to see the cosmos through astral projection or lucid dreams was long forgotten. I now lived my life according to Syd Barrett and often found myself thinking, "What would Syd do?" For those who don't know Syd Barrett, he was the original lead singer, songwriter and co-founder of Pink Floyd. He was also known for his excessive use of LSD.

As eye-opening as this period of my life was, it had to come to an end. The psychedelic life-style was not for me, so I decided to look inside for my answers. I talked to many people at the spiritual church, who in turn introduced me to my first led meditation. This in itself opened up a whole new world of possibilities to me.

It was during one of these meditations that I remembered a book I had read years earlier. It had used Egyptian methods for astral projection and had briefly touched upon lucid dreaming. I had no idea where the book had gone but there was a slight possibility I had sold it for ganja money. Not to be discouraged, I headed off to the local library and what would be a new chapter in my life.

I never found the book I wanted on astral projection, but I did find a book on lucid dreaming and as it turned out, this was a great way to explore my subconscious mind. I think at some point lucid dreams and astral projection meet in the middle. This was the case for me anyway. The approach to enter a lucid dream was simple; I just recited a passage of text at regular intervals during the day. The premise being that at some point I would recite the same passage while dreaming, thus I would realize that I was in fact dreaming. In order to ensure I didn't forget to read the passage, I wrote it on my cigarette packs. Whenever I smoked, I read the passage.

This is what I used. You can use this or just about anything that will create a trigger.

Can I remember waking up this morning?

45

Is there anything here that should not be here?
If so, then I am indeed dreaming.
I can do whatever I want.
I can go wherever I want.
Where do I want to go? And what do I want to do?

It's no mind-blowing piece of literature but it is just intended to create that lucid moment.

So, why the purple parrot?

During my last two years of high school I worked with my cousin at his garage. I prepared cars for painting and performed standard services. It wasn't very lucrative for me but he listened to the same type of music that I did, he had the same name as me, which meant I rarely forgot it, and he was also married to my cousin. The garage was in a large building at the back of his parents' house. They lived in an old manor house on railroad lands that came with its own orchard. The garage leaked, was cold and carried an odor indicating its best days were behind it, but I loved it there. As time passed, I spent more and more time at the garage, so it came as no surprise that it was part of my first lucid dream. If you have ever managed a lucid dream then you will relate to the way I describe it. If you can remember the first time you watched a DVD movie after VHS worn tapes, this is how the dream was for me.

I was sitting at the kitchen table; outside was damp and overcast, a typical English spring day. My cousin was at the table reading a magazine on car modifications. His second cigarette of the morning burnt gently away in the ashtray as his attention focused on the scantily-clad models draped over the cars. His father flittered around the kitchen mumbling something about the cost of dog food while his mother prepared more cheese on toast. I looked out beyond the orchard and down the lane into the field behind the manor house. The hills in the distance caught some rain as the low-lying clouds passed by.

Returning my attention to the plate in front of me, my cheese on toast was just about ready to eat. The cheddar had cooled enough that it would not cause blisters. Yes, it had happened to me on more than one occasion. It was right at that moment when I started to recite the passage.

"Can I remember waking up this morning?"

As soon as I spoke the words, I felt an immediate change. It was almost like a fog started to lift and the kitchen became a sharp and clear image.

"Is there anything here that should not be here?"

I was getting embarrassed now. I was very conscious that I was saying these words, but I could not stop. My mouth had a mind of its own, what was wrong with me? This was almost like the time I tried the legal weed salvia, and all it did was make me drool and laugh uncontrollably.

As I looked around the kitchen, everyone continued what they were doing, oblivious to my ramblings. With the words "Is there anything here that shouldn't be here?" still lingering on my lips, a large purple parrot appeared through the far wall. It slowly flew across the kitchen, the action of the wings disturbing the fine column of smoke from the cigarette in the ashtray as the parrot continued through the wall and into another part of the house.

It was at this time that my dream stood still. I was in a dream but awake, I was scared, excited and really didn't know what to do. I had wished for this moment so many times, but I froze. There were a million things I could do, but as the moment presented itself, I was unable to think of a single one. I sat in the kitchen, nursing my cheese on toast. The dream world as I knew it continued. The hills still caught the rain, the garage still leaked and my journey to the cosmos was about to begin.

Unlike most other things I try, lucid dreams have been a constant through my journey. I did manage an OBE through astral projection but once I had achieved it, I no longer had the urge to try it again. Lucid dreaming offers me a chance to chat with my subconscious self. I used this method to construct a Gandalf-like tower where I could write in my grimoire and practice spells and rituals within a safe environment. I developed the Secret Garden meditation the same way.

There are obviously some things everyone thinks he or she will do when a lucid dream is achieved. Spending the night with your favorite crush, or flying through the sky like Superman seems so frivolous when you are actually there. Take the time to spend a moment with yourself, expand your horizons. Who knows where you will go? Perhaps we will meet in the cosmos one day.

So what did I take from this?

The green light didn't really work. I was likely just baked all the time, but there really was something to this lucid dreaming. For me it was almost like an affirmation of what is possible. If you are an Aries you will get this right away, but all too often we start something with no real plan on how we will complete the task because we quit before we have even begun. Lucid dreaming is something that we can achieve in a relatively short space of time with very little effort, but it offers so much.

If you can expand this concept into astral projection then you are only limited by your own thoughts. I have managed to experience an Out of Body Experience on two occasions but each time I was startled and returned to my body very quickly. The method I used had its footings in the Egyptian culture but there are many ways you can achieve the same result. If you want to attempt it using the method I practiced, then here it is.

Find a comfortable place to lie down. I chose my bed, but if you do the same, please make sure you don't do this when you are going to bed as it will most likely put you to sleep before you achieve an OBE. I speak from experience. So let's assume you are all lying on your beds, the curtains are drawn, the door is closed, and you are in a quiet relaxed state.

Starting with your feet, let go of any stress in them and allow them to relax. As they release any tension, they should begin to feel heavy, pulling them deeper into the bed. Move up your legs, relaxing and releasing tension as you go. Next, relax and release tensions in your hands and arms before moving onto your torso and finally your head. Take your time to do this; rushing at this point will only be detrimental to your own experience. If you have done this correctly, you should now be free from tension, and fully relaxed. Your body is so heavy it is difficult to move as you feel rooted to the bed.

Imagine yourself inside a pyramid. It is quite a large pyramid with the four sides extending hundreds of feet above you. It's light enough to make out the smooth sand-coloured surfaces as they merge into the perfect peak far above you. Lying on the floor, staring at the peak, a faint sound threatens to break the silence. It is a pulsating sound that begins to fill the pyramid with energy. As the sound grows in strength you feel the waves of pulsating sound fill your body as you become one with the pyramid. A small doorway opens in the top of the pyramid offering a glimpse of a bright blue sky beyond. Still lying, you feel yourself slowly start to rise. As you do, you repeat this following passage until you reach the doorway. There is no set number of times you must repeat this, the speed of your ascent is completely up to you. I normally spoke it three times.

Hear me Anubis and Nebet,
Though guardians of the astral plane,
I command thee to grant me free
And unobstructed entry into thy domain,
So that I may become invisible to others.
The glory of Osiris commands thee,
So shall it be forever more.

Once you reach the doorway, rotate until you are facing the sky beyond. Slowly edge out through the doorway and begin your astral journey. On both the occasions I managed to complete this without falling asleep I found myself back in my bedroom watching myself as I slept. This in itself can be quite disturbing and can trigger a recall response, but when I was faced with a tall person of seemingly Egyptian descent peering at me from the corner, it was enough to immediately startle me back into my body. I am not vain enough to assume that I was visited by an Egyptian god, but the presence felt as real as any interaction I have experienced within my waking life.

You can use any passage you like, the ones here were compiled from a number of ideas that I took from the years of study and research.

I wish you happy and safe travels.

Celestine

Here I was again, online dating. It was like a damn meat market, how did I end up here? Things had changed during the years that I had been out of the game as they say, and I really was not prepared for the aggressive pursuit of companionship. The one bright spark was the requirement that I had to create an online profile. I am not quite sure why so many people balked at this part of the process for I loved it. Never one to pass up an opportunity to talk, or better still, to talk about myself, creating my profile was just like an uninterrupted conversation with an attentive audience.

Eagerly I threw myself into my online persona with an earnest abandonment of the truth. If I were half the man I described, I would possess the patience of the Dali Lama, the wisdom of a lifetime's pursuit of enlightenment and the ability to wear the orange robes of the Buddhist monk, and make them look good. I may have gotten slightly carried away, which became apparent when I was faced with the option of either reducing the content in my profile or opening a second account just to continue. With the second option seeming a little crazy and maybe a red flag for some people, I opted to edit my profile to fit within a single account.

It didn't take long to start getting responses to my profile. Some women actually wrote to me just to thank me for the read. They didn't want a date; they just wanted to read my profile. This was in stark contrast to the guys, as they tended to skim through the profile to the bikini shots before writing to just about everyone. I guess when you throw enough mud at the wall; some will eventually stick. It's a numbers game. I even came across women who placed a secret word at the end of their profiles and would only respond to people who actually read the full profile and included that secret word in the email. Include it, omit it, wink, poke, nothing was really working for me.

I was even considering creating a female profile so that I could wink to myself, a sort of Phillip experiment within the dating scene, but that's the sort of red flag there is no coming back from. Besides, what if I wrote to her, to me, and I, me, didn't write back? I couldn't handle that level of rejection.

Having used Facebook more and more for social connections, against my better judgment I signed up on a free dating app. I say it was free, but it did require I enter personal information, just "for my profile." I would not have bothered but it was the sister site to one of the main ones I had already signed up for, so I figured what could it hurt?

My only cause for concern was the fact they again asked for my credit card. I really didn't trust these sites, and diligence when it came to my credit card statement was never really my forte. That was until one day, purely by chance, I noticed around twenty payments to a grocery store in Poland. I am pretty sure I would have remembered flying there to pick up a jar of pickled lamb's gonads, that's something one would typically recall. Evidently my card had been compromised during the process, which I promptly cancelled but never did receive the gonads.

Prior to the gonad incident, my accounts were active for three months. During this time I conversed with some characters, well let's just say I must have lived quite the sheltered life, but I also experienced some real connections. There was one particular woman whom I would frequently see online. This makes it sound like I was parked on the web site just waiting for any poor female soul to stumble upon my profile, which was not the case at all. It seemed like we would both logon at the same time, hang around for a few minutes then logout. After a week, I sent her a wink and to my surprise, I got one back. This was different and caught me off guard. Perhaps she clicked on the wink button instead of the "Run for the Hills" button by mistake as it seemed to be the only option on my profile.

"Hiya," I said, half-expecting to see her immediately pop offline.
"Hi," Rebecca replied.

This was great, an actual response, and it was obviously not a mistake. I make myself sound far too desperate; I was a catch! That's what my platonic friends kept telling me anyway.

This was quickly becoming quite the strange relationship, even for an online one. I would always seem to logon during the few minutes she allowed herself to chat on the dating sites each day. It really didn't seem to matter what time of day it was, we always seemed to bump into each other. Our conversations comprised of mainly one-line questions and answers which led to a surprising strong connection, though I wasn't quite sure where it was going to lead.

Back on the regular sites, things were not moving quite as quickly as I had envisioned. As the days passed, it became apparent that I was being approached for spiritual guidance more than the regular chitchat expected from the online dating scene. If it was just the one site, I could have put this down to coincidence, (though we all know there aren't any), but this seemed to be a common request across all the sites I frequented. To be honest I was beginning to feel like a spiritual "Dear Abby" bereft the inherent benefits that position would command. No word of a lie, I actually went through a thirty-day period that saw me help thirty women resulting in no dates what-so-ever for myself. That had to be some sort of record and it certainly left me questioning myself along with the profile picture I had chosen for these sites. Speedos were still cool, weren't they?

What has this to do with Celestine?

The underlying message of *The Celestine Prophecy* was that there are no coincidences. I did not see how this had any connection with my current situation until the last day I spoke to Rebecca. I didn't see it at the time, but I had lost all interest in the online dating scene with the only real light at the end of the tunnel being the help I was providing on a daily basis. It was quite an eye-opening period as I learnt some valuable lessons and understandings that would go on to help keep me in good stead within my own relationships. It was all very symbiotic with me passing on spiritual thoughts and discoveries in return for validation in my own abilities and empathy for the unheard. I was convinced that this was the sole reason I was still using the sites, this and my unhealthy need for constant attention, albeit through a bloated and self-maligned profile. Had I known how this was all going to end, would I have still spent all this time helping women date other men while I paid for the privilege to do so? Who knows, but as it happened this all culminated in a surprise reading one late night.

It was after ten and I was already tired. I had promised myself an early night and was about to turn off my computer when I got an Facebook message. It was Rebecca. She must have been creeping my Facebook account as she started to question me about the paranormal events I had posted. Although we had skirted many subjects over the past few months, I had purposely steered the conversations away from the spiritual or paranormal. The reasons for this should be obvious; thirty days, thirty women and no dates, there was no way I was exposing Rebecca to that part of my life. With the nature of her inquiry, I could already see this was only ending one-way, sigh.

My heart sank as she asked her next question.

"Can I ask you a spiritual question?"

The anxiety knot in my heart chakra was the telltale sign that a message was coming through. Having grown accustomed to this feeling, I acknowledged the rule of first thought and opened my mind to what information would be sent through. It was at that time I received a download of memories and insights related to Rebecca and her life. This was typically how my guides corresponded with me. All I had to do was put them in some sort of order and make some sense of them. We began the impromptu reading and as it turned out, each time Rebecca asked me a question, it triggered certain memories, thoughts, and emotions that made it quite easy to provide seemingly insightful responses. After two or three hesitant and vague questions where I was very specific and to the point with my responses, she asked me if I was psychic. I had been somewhat at an advantage given the information I received so I was my customary sheepish self when I finally admitted that I might have a tiny amount of skill in that area.

The reading continued for over two hours and produced many tears with moments of joy and discovery. As we were closing the reading, I was asked to mention meditation to her. This was met with silence. Without even realizing that I received the information I typed,

"It will help with your addictions."

This triggered another bout of tears but not through embarrassment or guilt but more because of the recognition that only a non-judgmental acceptance can provide. We covered many topics that evening and even communicated with her daughter's spirit guide which I am sure was more for me than it was for her. Her sister was involved at some point, her daughter at another and we really seemed to help mold a life's plan for Rebecca and her family. For the first time in a very long time, she had a direction and the inclination to follow it.

This was one of those life-changing readings for all involved. If I had to pick one impression from the reading that stood out for me, it would be Rebecca's daughter's spirit guide. She was an older woman, almost like the stereotypical grandmother but she looked like she could outrun me. She was short, in good shape and had a smile that enveloped you in peace. What struck me more than anything was her hair. The grey and white curls nestled on her shoulders shone with the vibrancy you would expect to see in a six-year-old girl. It was remarkable.

As we were saying our good nights, I was shown the *Celestine Prophecy*. Not one to really put pressure on anyone to go out and buy any particular book, this instantly resonated with me and I knew what it meant. I was given visions of Rebecca missing major crossroads in her life, too many missed opportunities, no direction and this had to change. I told her that there was more and proceeded to explain how the *Celestine Prophecy* had helped me and how I believed it could be beneficial in her life. She needed to learn how to recognize when the universe presented her with opportunity; there are no coincidences.

I was shown the book twice so I knew she had been asked to read it on two occasions, which she acknowledged. I asked her why she hadn't read it. She had no real answer, just a lack of enthusiasm to try anything. Given past and previous choices she had made, it was easy to understand her apathy. I urged her to get a copy and really try to commit to reading the book.

We talked for a few more minutes and I again asked her to pick up a copy of the book. I even sent her a couple of messages on MSN before I finally drifted off to sleep. I don't know if it was because of the reading or just to shut me up, but the next day I received a message from Rebecca stating that she had in fact bought the book and had already started reading it.

That was the last time we ever spoke.

The next day I was making supper for myself in the kitchen when I felt someone behind me. Other than the five cats, I was alone in the house so I was somewhat alarmed. Turning quickly I was face-to-face with the daughter's spirit guide. It was only for a brief moment but it was long enough to again view those youthful grey locks and witness her loving smile. For me, this was a moment of thanks and validation. I never saw her again.

So, what can we learn from this?

I am not asking you all to rush out and buy *The Celestine Prophecy* but I will ask you to embrace opportunities as they are presented and act upon them. They are part of our life's dream for a reason. They could be lessons we need to learn or connections with another person that will open up new doors of discovery. The thing is, if you ignore them, you will miss them. The months of online chat between Rebecca and myself were no coincidence. The help I provided leading up to that reading was no coincidence. It held my attention long enough to ensure I was there when Rebecca was ready to receive her message. What happened culminated in a reading that changed three lives forever.

The more you recognize these opportunities, the more you will see them. The more you act upon them, the easier it becomes to explore the unknown. The beauty is that even if you have missed them all up to this point, we are blessed with a world that continues to present them. Open your eyes, thank the universe for them, for there are no coincidences.

I mentioned a time where I took comfort from the words of the book myself. I don't normally talk about my brother's passing but it does have a bearing on what we have just talked about. Part of the book describes how we all choose our lives and that déjà vu provides glimpses of our life's dream, a sort of check-in to ensure we are on the correct path.

I had read both the *Celestine Prophecy* and *Tenth Insight* weeks before I received the news regarding my brother's accident. I had a brief moment where I felt numb which was replaced with an empty sadness. I cannot explain it any other way, it's as close to a lifeless emotion I can really relate to. Within a few minutes I felt a tugging in my heart chakra and saw the *Celestine Prophecy*. It was at that time I recalled the chapter on life's dreams and how we make a choice based on the lessons or connections that life has to offer. If I knew this was going to happen and I still chose this life, then it would stand to reason my brother chose his knowing it was going to happen, but he still chose his, which brought me immediate comfort.

It occurred to me that sometimes we might be on a path not for ourselves but for other people in our lives. If we were always on our own path serving ourselves, then how could we be there for anybody else's? The next time things just don't make sense or you feel it is difficult to stay focused on your path, perhaps you shouldn't be, and perhaps you are there simply to provide the means for someone else to advance along his or her own path.

Flash Cards

I f you are anything like me, the most difficult part of a reading when I first started was the interpretation of what you saw or felt. We all have limitations and of those, our own experiences can be the difference between a great reading and a stab in the dark. We receive information in many ways; I myself get a download of memories from which I need to make some semblance of sense. I do get "live visions," for want of a better term, but those are more common when I find myself being prompted by them to give an unexpected reading. The memories that I do receive relate to my own experiences as they pertain to the person I am doing the reading for.

The essence of the memories is the same for me as they are the person for whom they are intended, but the content and composition can vary enormously. Imagine we are all looking at a photo of a family spending time on a beach. Some of us see the full scene where others see the lapping tide leaving patterns in the sand. Some see the sun creating magical shadows where others only see the crowd of people and the mess they create. The photo we see is based on our own memories or perception of what a day on the beach should be. The composition is the same, the content can change, but from this we must discern the message as it relates to the reading.

Confused yet? I was. This was the main contributing factor that had me doubt everything I saw, and allow the rule of second thought to influence my interpretations. It stayed this way until out of desperation, I asked for a simple approach.

It was a late winter's evening, the Toronto Maple Leafs had finally made the play-offs and I was quietly optimistic. For years we had to listen to "Mathematically we can still make the play-offs." Well, that year against all odds, the mathematicians were correct and there I sat, testament to that statement. It was the first period and I was asking myself why I did not stop at just four slices of pizza. Setting goals in life is important, challenging yourself to eat an extra-large pizza before the first period ends really should not be one of them.

With the taste of Pepto-Bismol and root beer lingering on my lips, I gently swayed back and forth on the couch as the pain from a gallbladder attack ebbed slowly from my body. It was at this time when I started getting that telltale feeling in my chest informing me that something was coming through. Half-hoping it was the memories of a nurse who specialized in reducing the pain from a gallbladder attack; I tried to make sense of what I was receiving. It was difficult. I was still deliberating if I should attempt the last slice of pizza, convincing myself that the pain had somewhat subsided, and now I had this to deal with. It was hardly surprising that given my distractions, my rule of second thought dominated proceedings. I was always saying to myself that we over complicate everything so with that in mind, I asked for a simple message, one word at a time. It came in the form of flashcards.

OT and *1.15*

No way. Seriously? I was not getting the time of a game-winning goal, this does not happen. My rule of second thought immediately tried to turn this into something relevant as I racked my brain for anything rational. I even mentioned it to my wife at the time, not for any sort of validation but more for proof, as I didn't even believe it myself.

To me, the rest of the game was really just something that occupied a few hours until they entered overtime. I don't think I saw much of the game at all. If I did, then I had no lasting impression but on a more important note, I did eat the last slice of pizza.

The game entered overtime. I was really nervous now. I had stopped caring about the outcome of the game in terms of how it would affect the play-off series; this was now all about one thing, the time of the goal.

During the second period of overtime, I watched the clock. One minute in and no goal, then a break-away. My eyes were focused on the clock; one minute ten seconds. Just then the noise of the crowd caused me to break my attention from the clock as I caught sight of the puck having beat the goalie glove side. It really was one of those moments where everything seemed to happen in slow motion. I looked at the clock. Eighteen minutes and forty-five seconds left in the period, they had scored at 1:15 into the second over time.

Now before you all go off and look for an OT goal at that time, I am not a hundred percent sure of the actual seconds, it was many moons ago, but they scored on the exact second I had seen almost four hours earlier. I was beside myself; I had nobody to tell this to and really, who would believe me anyway?

Over the next few days I tested the principles of the flashcards many times.

I discovered at times that I could influence the cards to display what I wanted or expected to see. This was the rule of second thought creating this false sense of reality. It was going to happen; I am still human after all. When this happened, I stopped and left it for a while, allowing my mind to settle before thinking of another topic to request information for. I found that the best approach for me was to clear my mind and let it come. It was often preceded by the anxiety knot in my heart chakra that I now associate with a message or download of memories to help with a reading. Following this, the flashcards would start showing me words, phrases or numbers or would answer mentally asked questions with a yes or no.

My next big test came via my ex-wife's son; he wanted to know his exam marks. I was too excited not to try this so I asked the question and waited for the answer. The first exam came back at eighty-six percent, the next fifty-three percent. Those are the only two that I received. We waited for almost two agonizing weeks for his results. When they came in; eighty-six and fifty-three percent. He had other marks but those were the only two I was interested in.

I know it sounds like a long-winded tale and too good to be true, but that is how it happened and how I discovered flashcard answers. I still receive them today but overlook them for the most part, though I am not sure why. Maybe I think I have evolved past them, or perhaps they are always trying to tell me things I don't want to know.

So what pearls of wisdom can we take from this?

Do not and I stress this, do not attempt to eat an extra-large pizza by yourself over any period, and certainly not within the first period of a hockey game, it is just never a good idea.

If you are just starting out and confused about the information you are receiving, try asking questions and request one word at a time. They want you to get it as much as you want it; it makes it far easier for both sides once you start accepting and acknowledging the information they pass on to you.

Meditation

I hated meditation. I practiced but for a long time I really despised it. It was manifesting as a stumbling block between my goals and myself. Through perseverance, I managed to make some headway, though I was hardly a master by any stretch of the imagination.

I first started meditation or at least research into the act, while I was a teenager. My friend's father introduced me to the first of many methods I would try. He had drastically changed his life, having lost his wife at a young age and was following a truly spiritual path. His life changes included hours of daily meditation where he held conversations with his body and the universe. I once asked him how he managed to quit smoking so easily and he responded that he held a conversation with his body and they came to an arrangement. I was not privy as to the content of this arrangement but true to his word, he never smoked again.

Back to the meditation. This method required three people, a comfortable chair and an open mind. I already thought of myself as open but I quickly realized I was far from open.

I sat in the chair and closed my eyes. One person stood behind me and placed their hands on my shoulders; the second person knelt at my feet and placed their hands on my knees. Being the typical teenager, I was hoping the person at my feet was his new girlfriend. I tried to sneak a peek but I was sure they would have noticed me so it acted as a distraction throughout the entire meditation.

As we progressed I was asked to imagine myself as a ball of energy filling the chair. I was then asked to expand the ball and fill the room before expanding beyond the walls and out into the night air. As the energy expanded and rose, I would see myself floating up into the universe, or this is what should have happened.

Instead, I started imagining that I was a large floating whoopee cushion after a long night of beer drinking followed by an overly spicy Indian curry. I did eventually get better which is evident in my future accomplishments, but on that particular evening, I must really recognize it as one of the worst meditations I have had.

As we closed the meditation I kept the whoopee cushion notions to myself and was pleasantly relieved to see it was indeed his girlfriend at my feet. Although this first experience wasn't what it should have been, it opened me up to the possibility of meditation and what could potentially be achieved through practice.

It was a number of years later that I revisited meditation as I looked to incorporate it into witchcraft and some psychic phenomena I was practicing. This time I was far better prepared for what was expected and you will be happy to hear that there was no sight of a whoopee cushion anywhere. I talked to many people at the local spiritual churches and read many books on the subject but in the end I did what felt right to me. I chose an Egyptian approach that saw me call upon the gods to help and protect me within my journey. As I practiced, I recognized the change within myself. It had a far-reaching effect upon my spiritual work and more importantly, the candle magic that had captivated me.

As my interest in magic, meditation, and psychic development gave way to girls, beer, and weekends out on the town; my practices and budding skillset waned along with my piggy bank. It was not until almost ten years later would I once again pick up the gauntlet and set forth to slay the beast that was meditation.

I was embarking on a new journey, one into the paranormal and the darker side of the spirit world. Along the way I had met other investigators who were accompanied by psychic mediums. I had always had a sixth sense or the ability to see things in my mind but just figured that I was a damn good guesser.

When I was around eight-years-old, my cousin who was quite a lot older than me said I was very astute. Being an eight-year-old, he could have been talking a foreign language as that meant nothing to me, but I just smiled and said,

"I know."

So here I was again, sitting on the floor, my backside as numb as an ice sculptor's index finger and my mind as active as a very active activity that requires a great deal of active thinking. It was going to be a long road but I would get there in the end. I actually had no choice as my legs had cramped, preventing me from getting up. That allowed me ample time to lament on those weekends out on the beer instead of being home practicing.

As my skill returned, I found it easier to focus, or not to focus. I was able to quiet my mind. During one particular chakra balancing meditation, I found myself in what could be only described as nowhere. It was strange. I knew I was there which was nowhere, and I knew I was thinking about nothing, which in itself was a thought. It was definitely a Monty Python moment for sure. So there I was, sitting or floating in total darkness, no feelings, no thoughts, and no recognition of light or sound; just nothing.

Did I fall asleep? I still ask myself that today but I honestly cannot answer that. It is possible, I guess, but without anyone there to witness it, how could I know?

If I fall asleep during meditation and don't realize it, am I sleeping or meditating?

The only thing I can really be certain of is that I remember balancing my sacral chakra and in what seemed like the next moment, I had moved on to the throat chakra. This was twelve minutes of seemingly nothing.

Didn't something like this happen in the movie *Contact*? When Ellie went through the machine, she spanned time and space to visit an alien life form in the guise of her father. Upon her return, the cameras had recorded eighteen hours of static helping to support her claims that she had indeed been on a journey. This was certainly not eighteen hours and I am sure did not include any interactions with beings not of this earth, but I did experience something and as certain as I am that it wasn't nothing, it was in fact nothing that I experienced.

The next time this happened I was running through the same chakra balancing meditation. I am not sure if it started at the same point but I again found myself in the nothingness. This time there was almost expectancy that I would experience this again and as such I was prepared for it and was more aware of my surroundings. Granted they were pretty sparse given I was in the middle of nothing, nonetheless, I was aware of this fact.

As I sat content in the emptiness I saw a red dot of light appear immediately in front of me. I could not tell how far it was from me due to the lack of anything to draw a comparison to. The red dot of light was growing closer or getting bigger again, it was difficult to know which. At that point I returned to the meditation and continued with the balancing.

I was getting pretty good at meditation by now. I had cut my chops as they say and was looking to broaden my horizons. I started to look around on the Internet for anything other than balancing my chakras. I was pretty sure I was quite well-balanced and really, how many times can you balance your chakras in a day. The world of meditation awaited me as I discovered methods from how to convince to your body to eat less food to meditations designed to stop your feet from smelling. I am not sure how effective the latter was, I have a feeling this meditation was developed out of pure desperation one winter's night.

I chose two meditations. The first was a past life regression and the second was a life's journey progression. Over a two-day period I tried both meditations and they were amazing. As with all meditations, I started with my trusted chakra balancing in order to provide balance and to raise my vibration. By completing this step, any subsequent meditations would be far more vivid and provide an almost lifelike environment. It allowed me to make a real connection with the meditation and the lessons learned within. I would recommend that prior to any specific mediation you should perform a chakra balancing meditation ahead of time. If you are like me, the resulting meditations will be like night and day.

The past life regression came first. As I progressed deeper into a meditative state, the words and music enveloped me. I always choose to wear headphones when meditating; they really help quiet my mind and allow me to maintain focus. Similar to the time I experienced the darkness of nothing while meditating, there was no gradual transition from the act of listening to the meditation to finding myself standing in a stone round house.

As I became more aware of my surroundings, the presence of two other people startled me so much that it forced me to waken from the meditation. I was actually scared, my heartbeat was elevated and I felt as though I someone had jumped out and scared me while I peed in an unfamiliar bathroom in the dark.

I sat there, the headphones half pulled from my head as the meditation continued. As brief as the experience was, I remembered everything. The way the straw felt beneath the heavy damp footwear I wore. The weight of the dank cloak tugged heavily on my shoulders as it hung down my back. The scent of musky earth and vegetables that had seen better days permeated my very being. I could still taste the smoke from the smoldering fire in the back of my mouth.

If that was all I gained from that meditation then I would still consider it a success, but there was more. When I first entered the building, it felt like the two people who were already embroiled in a discussion before I arrived actually felt or saw me. I think more than anything, that is what scared me the most and led to the premature return from the meditation.

Was I actually there?

Who knows? But given the reaction from the two other people in the round house with me, I swear they were turning to face me as I fled the scene. I never did attempt the meditation again, though after an experience like that you would think I would want to return every day. I can't explain it; I just lost the desire to try again. I have since lost the meditation but writing this book has kindled a desire in me. Perhaps I will visit them again someday soon and maybe I will hang around long enough to interact with them.

The second of the meditations was to forward life's progression. This was designed to expose you to your life's purpose, the reason you chose the life you currently live. I was expecting amazing results given the experience from the previous day. The taste of smoke from the round house was nothing but a memory, but the visions were as vivid and clear as ever. The more I thought about it, the more I convinced myself that I was actually there. Where was this new meditation going to take me? I was about to find out.

I completed my chakra balancing and pressed play on the progression meditation. No turning back now as I sat back in the armchair purposely placed to ensure the stereo was out of reach. The meditation played and took me to a place of relaxation.

Just as I had expected, the transition was sudden and jolting. The sounds of the waves and scent of the sea were unmistakable as I looked down at a beach that had no end in sight. The sky was dark and stormy but the light breeze brought calming warmth. My feet felt cool as I wiggled and buried my toes in the sand causing it to squelch up between them. The squawking sounds of seagulls introduced their presence behind a bank of fog that stood between the water and me. By this time I had forgotten that I was meditating, I was there. The only sounds I heard were those of the beach and a distant calling of my name from a cliff to my left. I made my way towards the cliff and the sound of my name though I don't actually recall the journey. I felt the ground beneath my feet transform from sand to gravel to grass with no visual sense of a single step taken.

As the summit of the cliff appeared, I made out a small circle of people sitting beside the cliff's edge. The beach now far below me, extended beyond sight but maintained a sense of closeness. Fog akin to that seen in old London town was as thick as pea soup and hugged the water, creating a misty barrier stretching high into the sky. I returned my attention to the circle of people before me. They were children; all smiling broadly and welcoming me with their unconditional love and trust. As I moved closer, a gap in the circle became more obvious. Not really knowing what else to do, I moved closer to the circle. I was becoming aware of my nervousness as I sat in the gap created by two young children. Peering around the circle with each face more welcoming than the last, my eyes moved until I met the gaze of the woman with long dark wavy hair sitting opposite me. My nervousness left. *Kathryn.*

It was at this time that my concentration broke and I returned to the familiar feel of foam padding on my ears as the headphones continued to deliver mystical panpipes. A tinge of disappointment served as a reminder of the cliff where I had felt such warmth and comfort, was not far behind me. I hadn't return empty-handed. I had received the glimpse of a vision, a vision of my life's dream and an indication of how I should spend the time I have this time round.

The circle on the cliff was both a healing and teaching circle with both Kathryn and me providing this to the children in the circle.

Although the circle comprised of all children, I never got the feeling that I would be limited to this demographic. I think it was just easier for me to accept within the meditation as the children portrayed an energy of innocence.

I often wondered about Kathryn. Was she a real person or just a representation of a similar companion within my actual life? I think perhaps the latter but I always wonder. I imagine her atop the cliff, providing healings and teachings to anyone who needs them. An empty place in the circle awaits my return.

Like the past life regression meditation, I never tried it again. It's as though once I saw my life journey, I didn't need to see it again.

Meditation can sometimes feel like a chore. It can be difficult and occasionally unobtainable. The skill and concentration required to visualize and put yourself there is not always possible for everyone. I struggled with my own focus and my mind's chatter but I also found the ability to work through these obstacles. It may be a long road, it may take a long time, but the first time you find yourself standing on a beach with the words of the meditation fading in your ears, it will all be worth the effort.

So strap on those headphones, settle your thoughts and let your mind take you to places you only see in your dreams.

What lessons can we learn from this?

If someone has the decency to introduce you to meditation, have the grace to commit to it rather than imagining yourself as a methane gas-filled rubber balloon.

Find a meditation that really resonates with you, for that is half the battle. Perseverance and the will to let go of the trappings of your daily routine can provide a true test of one's dedication, but work through it. In general it is not easy to reach a place where the meditation becomes a reality to you. Even today it is hit and miss for myself, but I continue to give myself that opportunity. All forms of meditation help you raise your vibration, opening you to possibilities and potential that may currently seem beyond your current reach.

It was through meditation that I eventually accepted my vocation and took the steps to help me advance my healing and mediumship skills. It's amazing how much clearer things feel once you find a path that allows you to be who you are and surround yourself with people who choose encouragement over abashment. So grab your headphones, load up a meditation and take the steps into a world of possibilities, a world of potential, a world that contains an unlimited number of cliffs; each of which has a place just waiting for you.

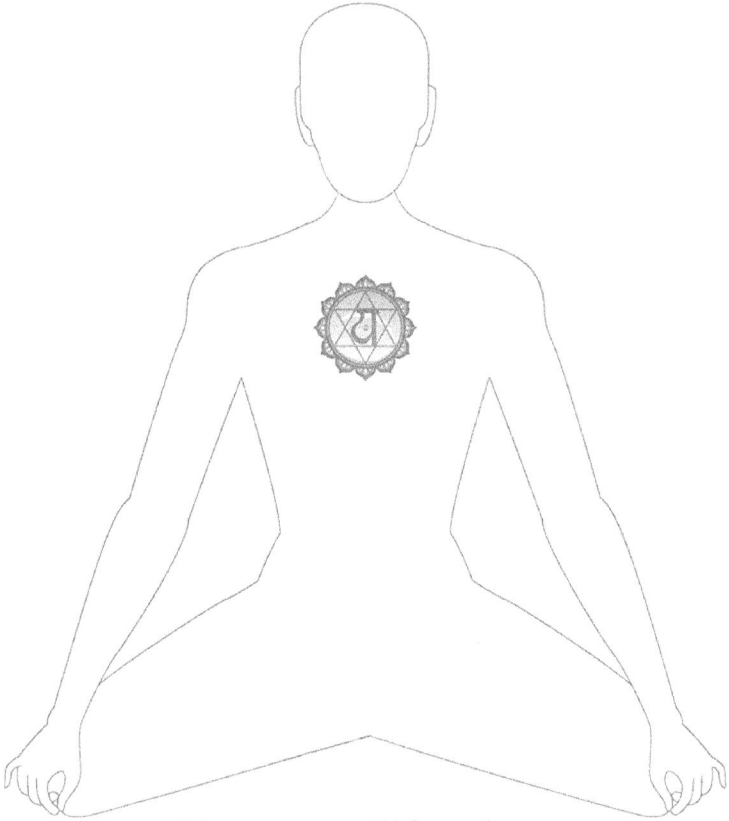

Heart Chakra
Anahata

LOVE

Anahata is symbolized by a circular flower with twelve green petals
called the heartmind.

Infinity and Beyond

The third and last time I used the Law of Attraction was just a few years ago. Many moons had passed since I had used this approach to obtain the refractor telescope and to be honest, I had forgotten all about it. I was reminded only after watching *The Secret* and thought, "Hey, this is just like what I did when I was a kid."

At around that time I had started looking for a new car. I owned a Saab Sedan, which in itself was quite a nice car, but I couldn't shake the feeling that it was an "old man car." As I didn't want to fall into a "my dad would like this car" trap, I thought a preemptive strike would be the best course of action, so I convinced myself that regardless of the impracticality, a two-door sports car was what I really needed.

I had one particular car in mind, a Nissan 350Z. My mind was set; it was going to be the growling beast with a manual transmission. For one, it made me feel empowered when dropping a gear and passing vehicles in a cloud of rubber. I later found out that this cost me about forty dollars each time. I never said my intelligence had improved with age. Two, my ex-wife couldn't drive anything but an automatic. Win, win.

Black was the colour or shade as it isn't technically a colour; black and chrome. I had the phone in my hand and was about to call when a friend of mine just happened to show me another car that I might like. An Infiniti G35 Coupe with the racing package. I didn't just like it, I LOVED it. That was the car I had to have, but looking at the fully-loaded edition with the racing package, the cost of this beauty was topping sixty to seventy thousand dollars. The monthly payment alone was going to be over eight hundred dollars a month. How could I justify this expense? I decided to let the universe decide for me. I calculated what was left from my salary once I had subtracted my regular outgoings and decided that anything less than five hundred a month would be acceptable. Given that was almost half the price these cars commanded, I did not hold out much hope that I would be driving one anytime soon. Regardless, I put my plan into action and once again turned to the universe to deliver the object of my desire.

I had been through this before so I somewhat understood the approach I had to take but given I had just watched *The Secret* I wanted to incorporate some aspects of that into my method. So began my third and final installment into the Law of Attraction.

I changed the desktop wallpaper on my laptop to a fully-equipped G35 elegantly presented by a scantily-clad young female model. When asked about the image on my desktop, I responded that it was my car, though to be honest, the majority of inquiries were regarding the said female.

When I drove the Saab to and from work, I imagined it was the Infiniti. The sound, the feel, the way it handled, everything but the miles per gallon that accompanied a twin-turbo engine, I put myself in the Infiniti.

I crafted an email outlining everything that I wanted in the car right down to the paint colour and concealed GPS screen. I sent this email to all Infiniti dealers within two-hundred kilometers and waited. I still continued to imagine that the Saab was the Infiniti, I even bought a clean car scented freshener to help visualize the new car interior. This went on for, yes, you guessed, two weeks.

Within the last few days of the two weeks, I received an email reply from a dealership in Newmarket. They had the last G35 in the province that matched the specs I had requested and with it being the demo car, I could have it for ten dollars less than I asked for.

Win, Win.

I kept the car for four years until a change in my employment reduced my commuting and retired the car to the driveway for long periods of time. It was a difficult decision but practicality prevailed and the car found a new home. I sometimes wonder what life had been like if had focused on the model on the desktop instead.

So, in conclusion, I have not used the Law of Attraction since that day. I have had my ups and downs and days that I really could have done with help, but I never really asked for it. I don't think there are any limits as to what we can ask for, but I do think that the more we ask the less our emotions and focus are associated with the request resulting in diminished results.

If you really want to try this for yourself I cannot stress how you must really BELIEVE that already you have what it is you are requesting. What I mean by that is, think of a time you really wanted something and then had the opportunity to own it. Think about how you felt the moment you knew it was yours, the time you unpacked it and used it for the first time. It is important you can recreate this emotion and associate it with the item you are requesting. If you simply wish you had something, you will always be wishing you had it. By acknowledging that you wish you had something, you reinforce the reality that you don't have it, this is the opposite to what you want to achieve.

Now the hard part. You must hold this belief and emotion for as long as it takes. It may only take a day or it could take months, there really is no definitive time that you can expect to hold this focus and emotion for, you get out what you put in.

Don't be disappointed if you don't get what you want right away. If it was that easy we would all be living on our own private islands by now. Maybe you were asking for the wrong thing or you need to be asking in a different way. Don't give up. Anything worth your attention and focus is worth waiting for.

Two Weeks

T wo weeks to what? I hear you ask.

Is this another one of those "11:11" or "12:12" things? Well, not entirely but who knows, they could be connected.

Over the years I noticed something. Apparently I have started repeating stories over and over while maintaining the same enthusiasm I had the first time I told them. The second is that apparently I have started repeating...oh damn.

Joking aside, the thing that struck me many moons ago was that no matter what I attempted spiritually, it took me around two weeks to accomplish my goal. It didn't seem to matter what it was; lucid dreaming, astral projection even meditation. From the moment I start it always seemed to take the same amount of time. So what is the significance of this? Well to me it is very significant. To you, not so much, but it is important you find your own two weeks.

Why two weeks?

I really have no idea. It could have something to do with my current spiritual journey. I say current, as I am a firm believer that we walk many journeys at any one given time. Over the years and lifetimes, our paths adapt to the choices we make. The destination may always remain as a fixed focus, but how we get there is really up to ourselves. Some of us get lost along the way, and we find ourselves continuingly bumping heads with the universe while some people experience the journey as a leisurely summer's day stroll. Don't you just hate those people?

So, armed with the knowledge that I can change the world around me in just two weeks, you would think I would be living the Life of Riley. I have often been asked why I have not experienced more success in life. Now, success can refer to many things. Am I living the life or walking "the path" I saw for myself? Have I amassed wealth enough to support a life-style of my choice? Did I find Waldo? And who the hell is Riley? All good questions and for the most part, the answer that always came to me was "I am not ready."

Using the rule of first thought, this was always the reply I heard before I took some time to look for an answer within myself.

Now, to throw out a blanket response like that is easy and some would consider it a cop-out. In part I guess it is, but by allowing that statement to answer some of my life's fundamental questions, is in itself a reflection of my current spiritual state. If I am to be truly honest, I am also a little lazy. There, I said it; I can procrastinate with the best of them. We all share similar lazy traits though many refuse to acknowledge them.

So if we are all this lazy, how do we get anything done?

Let me be clear here, I am not referring to daily chores. If you have been asked four times to take out the garbage as you lay on the couch watching sports while eating chicken wings, this is not a spiritual dilemma. The fact that you have one hand down the front of your sweat pants before you finally notice it was covered with Buffalo wing sauce but don't care, is a good indication that the latter is in effect, you are simply a lazy-ass.

I am referring to the times when we embark on a new spiritual journey. Being spiritual beings, we often think we should be doing more; we should be constantly involved in our growth. Again, not referring to the gain experienced through eating chicken wings, but the spiritual growth we experience through new encounters, thought processes, exploration and discoveries.

If you are finding it difficult to commit to a spiritual exercise, it could be an indication that you are not ready for it. You could push through but it often leads to half-hearted attempts where the recompense received is more from the actual act of participation rather than any spiritual growth. When you are ready, you will know.

So how does all this help me find my two weeks?

Pick an exercise you are comfortable with and set a goal for yourself. It is important that you truly commit. You only get out what you put in. Keep a diary and look for indicators supporting your success and failures. Yes, there will be times where you couldn't have been more committed yet the desired outcome eludes you. Look for changes in your surroundings, your spiritual patterns; even energy from those around you can affect your results. Just as commitment is key to these exercises, spotting patterns in your spiritual psyche is also crucial to sustained success and growth. Or, you could simply stumble upon those patterns as I did; it only took me forty years, how long do you have?

Obviously, this is all theoretical, I can only comment on observations within with my own experiences. The two weeks may be in part due to past lives and the levels of accomplishments within the various spiritual areas I attained within those lives. I believe that those skills stay with us; we just forget how to call upon them. When I again turn my attention to these skills, there is a period of two weeks of familiarity that I go through as I draw on my past accomplishments. It's almost like muscle memory, it never forgets. It just sits dormant until it is called upon. The time it takes to awaken is based on the amount of time I exercised the muscle and what level I achieved. It's just a theory of course.

Now, to the question of why am I not living a life of Riley?

Once I have accomplished what I set out to do, I lose all interest. It is as though I have a moment of inspiration or an overwhelming urge that drives me, and once I have achieved my goal, I move on to something else. Perhaps this is just a spiritual pit stop where I remind myself that these skills and lessons are as much a part of my current life as they were during lives where I acquired them.

Despite the amount of success I have had, I still have my own doubts. This is often what leads to a conversation I have with the universe prior to embarking on anything that relies on an interaction between myself and what I imagine the universe to be. Typically a one-way conversation, I state that upon receiving success, I will no longer doubt the universe or my part in its journey. Well, not until the next time anyway…

So what did I learn along the way?

Don't be afraid to fail, some of the most wonderful things are derived from happenchance.

When we really break it down, what is failure to us anyway? It's nothing more than an unexpected outcome to a desired effect. It's not wrong; it's just not what we had in mind. Participate, observe, and acknowledge your successes AND perceived failures; you will find your two weeks.

Duncan

Being a medium, psychic, or whatever mantle you associate with communications with spirit, has its challenges. Believe it or not, one of the hardest hurdles to overcome is our own ego. We like to think we are infallible, above it all, but it's not the case. We are still human and all crave and flourish when receiving praise and recognition. It affects some more than others and can stifle your progress like a kryptonite kick to your psychic butt.

Validation is the essence that births drive, focus, and belief.

The first step is to take a leap of faith and start to communicate your thoughts and feelings. Now this can be tough and it helps if you are within a circle of friends or family who will listen without judging, and encourage without validation. I was lucky to have such a group of friends around me and chose one liquor-laced evening to open those channels of communication.

For some reason I was drawn to a young woman from our group more than anyone else. This was not down to thoughts of attraction or anything sexual, there was just a stronger connection between the two of us. I had been receiving visions of her apartment for a couple of hours but said nothing as we all discussed our day-to-day lives and what we do outside the paranormal group activities.

Having plucked up the courage to be wrong, I asked her if I could share my visions in the hope that she could validate some of them for me. Thus began the night I gave my first reading. For my first "did I say that out loud?" reading, we would begin with her kitchen. I know right? Her kitchen. Honestly.

Now when I say I see visions, it's almost like they are my own memories. Luckily for me there is an indication that I will be receiving something as I get that telltale feeling in my heart chakra indicating that I either ate too many tacos or spirit is trying to communicate with me. It's as though I get a download of information in the guise of my own memories. I don't typically see the person receiving the reading within those memories, as they relate to my own life and experiences. My job is to take those new memories and apply them to the associated knowingness of the reading at hand.

The first thing I noticed about her kitchen was that it was very narrow which I considered to be more akin to a galley kitchen. This hit a chord right away with her as the superintendent had informed her of this not more than two days prior to this evening's impromptu reading.

Feeling more confident, I continued to describe what I saw. The clean finishes and hard lines reminded me of an IKEA showroom. The apartment itself was quite small; I felt confined, almost claustrophobic. Amongst all the whites, pale blues, and creams was a shining beacon of colour. A vibrant red glass vase was proudly displayed on the coffee table.

She was genuinely impressed and maybe a little spooked by the accuracy of my reading. As we continued to discuss what I had just shared, the group slowly turned their attention to me. She confirmed my vision right down to the red vase that tuned out to be a red wine bottle in the shape of a cat, but hey, I am only human. If this was all I saw, then it surely was a successful foray into the psychic world, but there was more. I received a vision right out of left field, and as random as you could get given the strange cocktails I had invented that evening. As we sat chatting I plucked up the courage to undermine everything I had successfully shared and asked.

"What is with the dirty socks in the drawer?"

She first looked at me as though I had spiked her experimental vodka and chocolate cocktail. Then her face changed, displaying a mixture of both disbelief and fright.

"Oh my god, how could you know about those?" she exclaimed as she covered her mouth with her hand in a display of shock.

I was now reveling in this. To get something as random as that must mean I am on the right track, right?

It turned out that she had been cold and put on two pairs of socks while she prepared and ate supper that night. Before leaving to join us she removed the second pair and tossed them into her sock drawer as she had figured nobody would know about them.

I continued to enjoy a strong connection with her and was able to develop my phone and online readings before an increased dependency on these visions began to generate concerns.

As our spiritual union developed along with our friendship, guidance on her life's decisions also evolved. Within the success I was experiencing through our connection, my own appetite for validation and expectations also grew. I was putting increasing pressure upon myself to deliver messages that were bigger, more momentous and had that "KAPOWWW" effect. This wasn't me, it was not who I was, this was my ego at work. I wanted to be the rock star psychic, *The Johnny Depp of the Psychic World*, or to be honest, just Johnny Depp. Luckily for me I witnessed how a tiny moment could have far-reaching effects early enough in my psychic career, that it brought me back to earth and help put things into perspective.

Heading to the séance, I was feeling a little nervous. The psychic who had been mentoring me was going to be there and I just knew she was going to ask me to participate, or worse, do a reading. I didn't feel ready; it was as simple as that. Through my life many people have asked why I am not rich given all the ideas I have. I simply reply, "I guess I am not ready."

This is not the case when I enjoy my own company. During meditation I feel as though the universe is there for me, all I have to do is reach out and connect with what I need. I am comfortable when it's just me. It's other people who make me nervous and cause me to second-guess myself. Maybe it was not them per se, but the expectations I placed on myself to provide an accurate message. Without them there are no expectations other than the ones I bestow upon myself. I just did not want others to witness my fallibility.

It was St Patrick's Day. I sported the green t-shirt that had been bought for me specifically for this event, but chose to pass on the plastic green leprechaun bowler hat. This party would comprise of a social mixer followed by food and non-alcoholic beverages before concluding with two séances. Given the diverse group we have, vouching for every member is simply not possible. This would offer some explanation into the not-so-subtle scent of alcohol in the air. Contrary to our fears, this presented no immediate concerns as everyone seemed comfortable and enthusiastic.

We had booked an old building in Toronto that used to house munitions during the Second World War and came equipped with its own walk-in safe and the largest and heaviest steel door I had ever seen. The energy in this old historical building was infused with an air of excitement that was not seemingly restricted to the living attendees we invited. Perhaps it was the anticipation of what was to happen, or the onset of heat stroke as the attendees who opted to wear the green plastic hats began to perspire. Either way, I was still getting nervous.

As the host, certain things were expected of me, mingling being one of them. Now anyone who knows me will attest to the fact that I would never pass up an opportunity to talk, especially when it comes to my favorite subject, me. I tore through the group like a spectral whirlwind, albeit, a very talkative one. As I met each person, my psyche began to react to the anticipation and growing energy generated from fifty like-minded people.

The party did not run as long as we had planned, though the food was consumed at an alarming rate. I can only assume that to stand in a somewhat cramped space wearing a plastic green hat increases one's appetite. It was that or the majority of people who forwent alcohol on the holiday that was specifically created to drink green beer, opted instead for the old leafy green stuff leading to what was commonly known as the munchies. Either way, we slowly began to occupy the vacant seats around the room as the two makeshift circles took shape within the loft. The lucky ones found one of the seats scattered around the room while the rest found an open space on the floor. I was in the latter group.

I lowered the lights, lit the candles, and took my place in the outer ring at the far corner of the room.

There were a number of psychic mediums present that night and each of them had amazing tales of little old ladies or angry gents walking the corridors of this historic building. For me, it started slowly. A single word. I listened to my mentor describe the old lady who was with us. She described what she wore and went into great details about her life. I was so jealous. Why did I not see any of this?

I closed my eyes and tried to see, to see anything and there it was again. The same word. Over and over, the word flashed in my mind on a flashcard. It was relentless.

Another psychic was taking his turn and told a tale regarding the older gent who walked the corridors and stairways of the building. He has been here for many years and was employed during the Second World War to work in the armory. I listened as I attempted to change my focus onto anything other than the word. If I ignored it then perhaps something else would come through. I opened my mind and put my trust into the rule of first thought. There it was again, and that time the word was capitalized.

The first séance was winding down and I was relieved that I had not been called upon. What did I have to say anyway? One word?

We remained seated in our circles; nobody had really broke formation though many of those without a chair shifted to find a more comfortable position. The hard wooden floors, as beautiful as they were, offered little comfort and were unforgiving to our numbing derrières despite the distractions we had all shared.

I sat quietly, hoping nobody would ask me to talk about my experience. I felt sick, just like the time in Vegas when my colleagues joked that they told the ticket office that it was my birthday as we made our way into the midnight review show. I was convinced that I was going to be called up on stage in front of thousands amidst bare breasts and feathers. It ruined the show for me.

"Gary." The voice of my mentor echoed around the high-ceilinged room, bringing me instantly back into the present.

"Gary? Did you get anything?" she asked.

The room fell instantly silent as the chitchat regarding the lack of alcohol was replaced with genuine interest as everyone turned in unison to face me.

I heard my own voice before I realized I was talking.

"I just got one...word..." I said, pausing out of fear of ridicule. "Duncan," I finally blurted.

The wide-eyed group expecting a wondrous tale of past lives, quickly lost interest and continued with their conversations regarding the green beer that was on tap at the bar down the street. Everyone save for one person.

Little known to me, a woman who had travelled from Barrie had requested a sign that night. She had followed a spiritual path for a number of years with little to no affirmation but before leaving for the event she had put out a challenge to her spirit guide.

"Give me a sign tonight or I am going to forgo this journey."

The name of her spirit guide was Duncan.

She quickly found me as the circles dispersed and we gingerly got to our feet. With feeling once again returning to our nether regions, she recalled her journey and how she almost fell off her chair when I spoke the name of her spirit guide. We have been great friends ever since and I have to say, she is such a wondrous spirit. She has grown far beyond that night and is a practicing medium, a student of physical mediumship and attends workshops all over the world. I am sure she will go on to do amazing things as her journey takes her far beyond her dreams from that night.

It was not a reading packed with heroics or momentous discoveries, but a vision containing a single word.

On that night, "Duncan" had the power to change a life, the wisdom to validate it, and the innocence to keep it true.

What did I learn from this?

Humility.

This lesson could not have come at a better time for my psychic journey as I was heading down a path that would surely have ended in a bad place. My ego was very much out of control and I have no doubt that I was pretty obnoxious to be around. The problem with always looking to one-up yourself is that you run the risk of searching for information or embellishing what you receive in order to present a picture far more grandiose than intended. This will not lead to a path of service for others but one of self-service. Ditch that meddlesome ego, concentrate on one word at a time, and the sentences will take care of themselves.

I did say we had two séances that night so it would be remiss of myself not to mention what transpired during the second. We have established the lesson I took from the evening focused on the single word I received but the second séance presented another milestone in my psychic career.

With the food reduced to mere scraps, many of the attendees began to filter out not long after the first séance. Within a short space of time we found our numbers had dwindled to less than twenty which suited me as it meant there were now fewer expectations. With enough chairs to cover the remaining partygoers, we decided to push the tables together creating a long singular table of various heights.

As the séance began, I instantly made a connection with a woman who sat at the far end of the table. This caught me off guard and I went to second thought in an attempt to rationalize what I was seeing.

At this time I did not understand how I received the information; it was all very confusing for me.

With the majority of the people in attendance being friends, I decided to just share my vision. I began slowly with the introduction of a little boy who was five or six years of age. He was riding a small tricycle around the room oblivious to the adults sitting around the table.

As I described him, the woman at the end of the table acknowledged that she had lost a child fitting that description. The next vision I had was one of the child standing with his grandmother by a grave holding a stuffed toy. The validation that her son had been buried next to his grandmother and with his favourite toy, a stuffed rabbit, brought many around the table to tears. I had never expected to have anything validated, never mind something so personal. That vision was quickly replaced with one of him sitting on the table in front of his mother hugging her.

Given the experience we had all just shared, we had no reason to doubt this vision and his mother did indeed verify that she could feel him. This really was a turning point for me, though I still carry that lingering doubt that always keeps me humble.

Self-Belief

I was still not sure about this; I would be sitting amongst real psychics, what if I got everything wrong? The thought of going to Lily Dale was a double-edged sword for me. On one hand the chance to learn from Rev. White was an amazing opportunity, but in the other, I had not really done much in terms of exercising my psychic muscles, and this terrified me. Was I going to be good enough? Would the other psychics look down upon me or even shun me as a charlatan? I feared and resented them before I even knew them.

The day of the trip arrived. Donning my lucky Metallica t-shirt I hit the road. Having read the *Celestine Prophecy* on a number of occasions I was always on the lookout for coincidences or the lack of, as the case may be, and that day was no exception.

The drive to the U.S. border was uneventful, the radio played quietly as I tried to envision how the week would go. As with most of the times I attempted to visualize a picture of how something will transpire, it soon morphed into a ridiculous scenario. I do tend to set myself up for a fall, which I guess is why I always try to see the worst case scenario. That way I am never disappointed. You may have gathered that I have somewhat of an overactive imagination that can be a real hindrance at times.

As I mentioned earlier, I am always on the lookout for coincidences, signs, déjà vu or just about anything I can pin my failures on after the fact. Going through the U.S. Customs was one big sign.

"Where are you headed?" the customs officer indifferently inquired.

"Lily Dale, it's in New York," I replied as I handed the officer a printed sheet that outlined the course I was taking, the address and the nearby motel where I was going to be staying.

"How long are you going for?" he asked as he scrutinized the paperwork I had just handed him.

"A week. Well unless I finish early, then I would be heading back sooner," I responded not wanting to elaborate but providing enough information to move this along quickly.

"So how long are you actually you going for?" he asked emphasizing the word "actually" enough to cause the couple next in line to peer in my direction.

"It really depends on the course and how it goes. It will be a..."

"How long?" the officer asked cutting short my response as he shifted in his seat.

"A week," I quickly replied.

"What are you going for?" the officer asked clearly irritated at this point.

"It's, urm, a medi, a mediumship course." I responded clumsily as sweat began to appear on my forehead.

"A what?" he exclaimed as he tossed the paperwork onto the desk and leaned back into his chair.

"It's," I paused. How could I explain this without it turning into a situation that would see me on my way back to Canada? "It's just like meditation. It's a place to meditate and expand your abilities," I finally blurted out.

"Can you not meditate in Canada?" he asked, clearly looking to irritate or goad me into a battle of wits.

"Yes, but this place has been around for over a hundred years, it's..."

"Are you going to work?" he again interrupted me as he began typing something on his computer.

"No, no sir. I am not working. I paid for the course," I replied as I urged him to pay closer attention to the documents strewn on his desk.

"You paid to meditate? Can you not do it for free in Canada?" he smirked obviously pleased with himself for delivering a seemingly demeaning retort.

"Yes, I suppose I could but I am also going for the experience." I responded with control. I was determined to take the high ground as you would when dealing with a difficult child at kindergarten.

This went on for quite some time before I was finally allowed to enter the U.S. and continue my journey. I actually had a conversation at Lily Dale later that day with a couple who had a similar experience with the same officer. The woman of the couple implied the guard was angry because he was so short. I am not sure that was the reason, but I took comfort knowing that I was not the only one who had wished him a *shart* at the worst possible time.

I made my way to registration at the Fire Hall and the location of my course. The encounter with the border officer weighed heavily on my mind. It was a sign for sure. I should not be here; the universe was making that all too clear.

I walked into the Fire Hall and into a wall of sweltering heat. The air-conditioner had packed itself in the night before causing the temperature inside to reflect the very thing the building had been erected to guard against. Sign number two. I hate the heat; and there was no way I could sit and sweat in the building for a week, my ass would be playing tunes every time I shifted in my chair. I must have looked quite concerned as a lady in a loose white robe smiled and introduced herself as she approached me. To be honest I was not paying attention, I really didn't want to be there so all I heard was,

"Air conditioner, broken, blah blah blah, Lyceum, you charlatan."

Okay, that last comment was my conscious mind making it uncomfortable for my subconscious mind, but where there's smoke...

Luckily for me my subconscious mind took control as I found myself back in the car navigating up a narrow road towards a building that was just coming into view, the Lyceum. As I entered the doors I was greeted with a blast of pure comfort. The cool air enveloped me, the heat and sweat along with the tense foreboding dissipated leaving behind a sense of calmness and optimism.

I still felt that I should not be there but at least I would keep the squeaky ass tunes to myself. I registered and sat for a moment in front of the empty stage. I closed my eyes and practiced some breathing techniques I had seen on an episode of *Friends* earlier that week. They didn't really help, but the thought of Jennifer Aniston certainly did.

The course was due to start shortly and other people began to arrive and find their place in the room. The chairs had not been allocated as such but small groups of people began to claim whole sections as they welcomed friends and acquaintances within their midst. I sat alone, my only camaraderie the dwindling squeak as I shifted uneasily in my chair, and the lingering scent born from doubt and my McDonald's breakfast.

We started slowly. Rev. White and the other woman explained how the universe around us was akin to the force from *Star Wars*. Let me stop here a second. *The Other Woman*. I feel terrible, but names are not my forte, which is why I usually call everyone Bob and Margaret. On one occasion the couple was actually called Bob and Margaret. It had to happen at some point.

So yes, back to the course. Some of the people sitting around me were receiving readings from Rev. White and the Other Woman. I patiently sat and observed. My uneasiness was still eating at me. "You're a fake." "What are you doing here?" "You smell like a fart." Just the regular banter we all enjoy with our malicious subconscious selves. Then it was my turn to receive a reading.

Oh no! All eyes were on me. Did I really smell like a fart? I shifted uneasily and basically nodded and smiled but heard very little of the reading. I got the general idea though. I was a druid high priest, and, blah blah priest, blah blah naked. What?!! Damn my subconscious mind. That did get me thinking about the reading though and why nobody ever seems to be that guy who runs behind the horse and cart shoveling the dung.

Readings over, we proceeded to begin our first workshop, Psychic Boot Camp. I felt sick. How was I going to pull this off? I had meditated a few times, made some well-founded guesses but psychic...Was I really psychic?

We arranged the chairs into two lines facing each other and took our seats. I had a feeling what was going to happen next but I was hoping it would be a game of patty cake or something. Not my luck, we were about to enter into the psychic equivalent of speed-dating.

"Okay. Everyone on this side will give a five minute reading to the person opposite," the Other Woman said, indicating that my row was the one to give the readings.

So this was it. Nowhere to hide now. It was just me, my psychic thoughts and the cute woman who sat opposite me. I won't go into details but I nailed it. I was so relieved I think I may have actually broke wind a little. I had survived. It must be my turn to receive a reading now. I took a breath and relaxed a little.

"Very good," the Other Woman said. "Now, the row who just received a reading, move down a seat. Those who just did the readings, a five minute reading for those opposite you."

Are you kidding me? I had just done my reading and really wanted to quit while I was ahead. This second reading was not quite as accurate as my first but still very respectable. The woman could have easily been the sister of the first woman I read for, and she validated a good sixty to seventy percent of what I saw, so I felt quite pleased with myself.

"Everyone done?" the Other Woman asked. "The same row move down one seat again and this same row will give the readings," she said indicating the row I sat in.

I was half-expecting it now. She must have known how I had felt and was doing this to weed me out of the group. That wasn't really the case but I am neurotic at the best of times, and suspected she was out to get me. The third reading was going nowhere. I sat opposite a guy who starred back blankly at me and I got nothing. No connection, no thoughts or visions. I just sat there staring back at him. She was out to get me. After almost the full five minutes, I blurted out, "Do you have a garden?"

"A garden?" he responded

"Yeah, a garden." I repeated as I lowered my head to stare at the floor. "Hasn't it been five minutes yet?" I asked loud enough causing those to my sides to nod in agreement.

"Okay, the five minutes are up. If you haven't finished your readings do so now," the Other Woman said.

I was so thankful; those five minutes had felt like a lifetime. Walking to the end of the line, the Other Woman turned to address everyone but focused her gaze in my direction; I knew it. She was out to get me.

"Sometimes you will not make a connection to the person you are reading. This is okay, it happens to us all. What is important is that you don't treat this as a failure; it was just not to be. When you experience this, try asking your guides a question."

She walked down the side of the chairs and stopped behind me. I couldn't see her but I knew she was there.

"We are going to try this one more time," she said as she gently put her hands on my shoulders. "This time if you don't get anything just ask. Now the same side move down again and this side will do a final reading."

She squeezed my shoulders ever so slightly before she walked back to the end of the line. Perhaps she wasn't out to get me after all, maybe she had picked up on my apprehension and just gave me the opportunity to prove it my myself. The line moved down again and I was relieved to see another woman opposite me.

I came to the realization during that week that I have a harder time reading men than I do women. I am not sure why. Perhaps I just find it easier to relax more when it's a woman and the primal urge to prove one's self as superior has been removed from the equation. I have since moved passed this, but at the time it led to a few sparse readings.

So for my fourth reading, I sat opposite a woman and was getting nothing. Bang goes my theory. I sat quietly for a minute and then I asked a question. I didn't ask out loud, that would be nuts. No, I asked mentally and didn't have to wait long for a reply. I was flooded with thoughts, memories and feelings; too many to deal with if I am honest. I did my best to make sense of them and it turned out to be an amazing reading. I was three for four, which was pretty good. Seventy-five percent and it could have been more if I had just asked a question when I did my third reading.

The rest of the week went swimmingly. I was certainly feeling far more confident, and dare I say I was even a little proud of myself. As the week progressed, people were actually asking me for advice, and it was amazing. I even felt like I belonged. I wasn't a fraud or charlatan; I just needed to believe in myself.

Now I know that the Other Woman wasn't out to get me after all.

So, what did I learn?

I would have thought that was obvious; my ass squeaks when I sweat. I jest but in all seriousness, self-belief or lack of it has cut short many a budding psychic career. Reminiscent to a virus, it spreads through your thoughts and encourages doubt over confidence and fear before courage. Most of the problems begin with an overactive sub-conscious mind, one that may have suffered setbacks or restrictions in the past. Those deliberations are where they need to be, in the past. The beauty about the past is that it can only affect your present and future if you allow it to. What has happened has already happened, there is no changing it no matter how much you wish for it. The future is unwritten; it is a constant clean slate that awaits your unique interaction. Belief in your own future is a belief in yourself.

I believe in my future. I believe that opportunity will present itself and I believe I now have the where-with-all to identify these opportunities and to act upon them. I believe this book will help people connect to a spiritual path they may have thought out of reach. In doing so it occurs to me, I believe in you.

Dark Stranger

This part of my journey is still an open book, pardon the pun. I would say that I my attraction to strange events or the darker side of life never really materialized into anything substantial until I started meditating for the second time. I never really took meditation too seriously until I moved to Canada. I was not against meditation; I was just never really a big fan of it. There was no specific reason for how I felt, or perhaps there was, but it was locked away in my subconscious mind.

A series of events eventually led me down the path to psychic development, but I was a reluctant psychic. Always self-doubting, always in some sort of agreement with the universe, it's surprising that I ever amounted to anything really, psychically speaking.

I tried a number of meditations, none of which produced much in the way of development. My third eye, as obvious as it may have seemed to be to other psychics, must have been pretty damned lazy because it eluded me.

I played at meditating for a long time. Most of the time I found it very difficult to "quiet my mind" sufficiently to achieve anything of worth. If you knew me you would understand why; my mind never stops. It's a hamster's wheel of ideas constantly spinning but rarely stopping to appreciate any of them. I fought the idea that I needed to meditate, but after substantial peer pressure I finally succumb to the idea and even built a room specifically for it. With the expression "you only get out what you put in" resonating in my overactive and noisy mind, I applied more effort and embarked on my new journey into my subconscious mind, and who knows what else.

Visualization is no problem for me; I can put myself into any situation and really feel the experience and emotion. You would think this would have obvious advantages during those mind-numbing hours while commuting into the city where I worked, but it often led to long periods of the journey where I have no recall what-so-ever. There must be an autopilot that kicks in and takes care of the driving for I don't think I have ever experienced one incident of road rage whilst in autopilot mode, and anyone who has driven with me knows that just simply isn't me.

So there I sat in the room I constructed specifically for meditating. The purple walls induced a spiritual comfort while the dark blue curtains and black ceiling offered an environment to expand my third eye. A small altar sat atop some old duct tape-capped water pipes that I was too lazy to fully remove. I am convinced that half the world would collapse if we were ever to experience the rapture for plumbing adhesive tape products.

As time went by, I managed to lessen the chatter in my mind. I don't think it will ever fall silent, but a slightly less audible cacophony was all I really needed. I started to experience some results, in particular with my ability to focus while receiving information from my spirit guides. With that success came the encouragement I needed to pursue it even further.

It was around that time that the paranormal group I was a member of organized a road trip to a location called "Ghost Road." It was a road of sorts, albeit loose gravel, but to brandish the road as haunted was simply an insult to ghosts everywhere. So there we stood, our digital thermometers drawn, the remaining meager supply of equipment shared between us as we fumbled around in the dark trying to avoid stepping on each other's toes. In our eagerness to obtain the cool gadgets as seen on TV, we may have overlooked some of the more practical items. Flashlights spring immediately to mind.

Not to let an oversight like that to spoil our evening, we headed up the road led by our intrepid leader, so voted because of the flashlight he had remembered. After a short time we covered the entire length of the road, and despite the lack of visibility, we suffered no mishaps. It was all a tad deflating if I allow my recall to see it for what it was. With the initial excitement over, the realization that they must have been muck-spreading earlier in the day began to dawn on everyone. I was actually blamed briefly but even I could not have produced such a penetrating scent.

As we made our way back down the road towards the cars, one member let out a cry of discovery. The spirit lights seen at the crossroads were nothing but an optical illusion caused by reflected car headlights on the nearby highway.

What? The ghost lights are not real? There was a real shocker. It was around that time I realized that I was quite the skeptic and that tact was actually not a skill set I had truly developed. This became more apparent as I fell into a comedic routine for the next two hours casting dispersions on the whole evening.

We visited the road on two more occasions, both times were during the hours of daylight. I am not sure why we returned; perhaps it was to convince ourselves that it was indeed haunted, or to find the lost ego of a couple of failed investigators. Whatever the reason, I was starting to enjoy being on the road; it did have a spiritual quality that appealed to me.

So why am I rambling on about a non-haunted road? Part of the meditation I had just started required me to select a location that would represent the road I would travel through for this particular journey. It would be my spiritual starting point and I could think of no better place than "Ghost Road."

I was five minutes into my meditation and it was going quite well. I stood on the road. It was a fall evening and the large red sun created long shadows as it slowly sank into the orange sky. The insects continued their choral song of retirement as I envisioned a large ball of energy moving slowly towards me down the road.

What happened next was completely unexpected and was not related to the guided meditation we were currently receiving from Rev. White.

As the meditation gave no indication that anyone should accompany me on the road, the presence of a man a short distance from me on the side of the road gave me cause for concern. Slouched against the fence with his back towards me, he emitted a strange energy making him quite difficult to read. As the ball of energy drew closer, he raised his hand and stopped it in its tracks. I tried again to pull the ball to me, but he held it fast. With his back still facing me, I approached cautiously. Even though this was a meditation and I was supposed to be in control, I felt a little uneasy.

Before I continue, I must describe the dark stranger. If you have seen Stephen King's *The Stand* with Rob Lowe, you will remember the blue denim-wearing devil. For those who have not seen it, he was around six foot tall, wavy hair to his shoulders, and unlike the fictional character from the book, this one was clad in black denim.

As I approached him, I moved to his right in order to get a better look at his face. It was at that time I realized that he had no face. Where his face should have been was a smooth egg-like surface but it was not the same colour as an egg. It resembled molten metal or the mercury found in older thermometers. I stood and stared for what seemed like just a couple of seconds when he suddenly began to make a really strange sound. It was almost trumpet-like but in the guise of a series of moans. As he made those sounds, he slightly tilted his head back, at which point I found myself back at my original position on the road. The dark stranger again stood to my left and continued to prevent the ball of energy from reaching me. As I composed myself and again concentrated on the ball, he released his hold and it slowly made its way towards me.

That particular meditation was intended to introduce me to a spirit guide via a journey within the ball of energy. The trip would see me transported to a meeting place somewhere between both existences where I would be met. As the ball came to rest in front of me, it filled my field of vision. At almost twenty feet in diameter, the ball pulsed from within, creating a slightly opaque barrier between the dark stranger and myself. I remained focused on the dark stranger as well as could be expected given my limited vision. His now pulsing image was slightly deformed. It was like I was peering through a substantial volume of water, and still he remained. A trespasser on what should have been my road of tranquility, my focus begrudgingly returned to my goal.

I stepped into the ball. It was quite large inside, much larger than it appeared from the road and was silent despite the continuing pulse that I could now feel as it washed through the inner surfaces. The ball slowly began to rise as we left the road surface, and then picked up speed as we cleared the treetops that lined the road. As I looked down, I saw the vacant face of the dark stranger following me until I vanished from sight.

I have seen the same stranger on three occasions. On all but one occasion he interacted with my meditation. I have never found out who he was, what he wanted or where he was from. Many people have offered theories but I am still searching for a satisfactory explanation.

When you meditate, try to open your mind to all possibilities. When we follow a guided meditation we tend to stick to what we are being told to visualize. That's not a bad thing; it just limits your possibilities. The next time you find yourself on a road while meditating, spend time to smell the roses and let everything just be.

So what did I learn from this?

It's hard to really pin down what I took from this. The dark stranger could represent a part of my life that sits on the fence between light and darkness. Maybe it's a symbol of obligations passed down to me through by-gone lifetimes and long lost relatives. Whatever the reason for his presence, what remains is the fact he is there and continues to check in on me from time to time. I take some solace in the notion that he could even be a visitor from another planet as I have been labeled a star child on more than one occasion. Perhaps he is just a figment of my overactive imagination, but I seriously doubt that. For one, he would have been a she, and she would have been wearing something far more fetching.

This is not the first time I have been presented with an opportunity to communicate through meditation only to be met by a faceless person. The very first time I tried a group meditation I found myself in what would become *My Secret Garden* and met what I could only describe as a wood elf who took great pleasure in jumping back and forth over the top of me as I sat on the fallen log. That person also had no face, but I still recognized them, if that even makes any sense.

When you meditate, continue to practice the rule of first thought. Allow those thoughts into your meditation; don't suppress them because they were simply not part of the meditation. All led meditations are designed for a wide audience and as such are very linear in their approach. The thoughts and visions you receive during these meditations are unique to you. Allow them to flourish and welcome them into your meditation. Perhaps there is a dark stranger waiting to communicate with you. Or maybe a being of light awaits you on your road of tranquility. Open your mind, your sight, and awareness and remember the rule of first thought; whoever you meet, you meet them for a reason.

An Apple a Day

As I do in life, I tended to jump around quite a lot during the writing of this book. Ideas would come and go, some would stay; others seemed just plain crazy after I had slept on them. This chapter on healing suffered from no periods of daydreaming or loss of direction as it is very close to my heart in more ways than one.

I have no idea how I started healing and did not believe I was actually doing it for a long time. I believed in the process but the results seemed too amazing to be real. How could they be real? Let me take you back to the beginning,

I was at Lily Dale studying psychic mediumship, and unbeknown to me this included healing and distance healing. I really had no interest in learning how to heal; I was there to become this amazing psychic who could talk to Elvis. I make light of it. Besides, with all the souls on this world why would he stop to chat with me? I don't even know half his songs. Regardless, I entered into our exercises with the commitment of a sloth, and as sloths go, I was slow even by their standards.

Sure, I would sit in the chair and get healed. Not that I have any ailments save for this boredom, but go for it. Return the favour? Sure. Why not? I waved my hands around like an inept magician whose sheer boredom was the reason the rabbit remained in the hat.

It was during one of those exercises that things began to change. As I took my turn in the chair, the people closest to me reacted to the energy I projected and commented on how it made them feel. This peaked my curiosity, but for all the wrong reasons. It had now become about me, not the healing, but how I was affecting the people around me. Now I was committed. We completed the healing and returned to the psychic circles. I much preferred those as I had developed a connection with two of the women in the circle that allowed me to easily connect with their energies, leading to very accurate readings.

As I left Lily Dale, all thoughts of healing quickly became nothing but a memory. It had been a fleeting curiosity born from my ego and one I easily left behind. I was destined for greater things. Healing was just not on my psychic radar. I wanted to talk to the dead. As I write this, I again come to the realization I did many years ago. I was an ass. I am not saying what I felt or thought was wrong, this was all part of my journey after all, but it still does not exonerate my ego or me.

So back to the day my healing story started. I have a real affinity to animals as anyone who knows me will attest to. This often leads to problems as I find it very difficult to walk by any animal in distress. There was quite the menagerie in my household with five cats, two rabbits, two rats, a bearded dragon, and a seven-foot iguana. As I said, I find it hard to turn them away.

I had just got off the phone with the vet; my youngest cat had a serious problem. Mickey was a two-year-old longhaired Maine Coon mix who was far too young to be this sick. Rescued from a home where he spent months alone, he had just started to settle in.

"It's going to be a one-way trip I'm afraid," the vet had said, lacking any form of emotion.

His words echoed through my very soul as I slowly processed the situation. How could Mickey's kidneys be failing? He had just turned two; he was so young and had his entire life ahead of him. Where were his remaining eight lives?

I sat in the basement lost in thought. Despite the sun having a few more hours in her, the curtains remained closed. I was already mourning my loss, but did it have to happen this way?

I was angry now; this was not acceptable to me. It was at that time I remembered my classes on healing at Lily Dale. It was crazy. I had dismissed the classes. I was no healer. I also remembered a reading I received during one of the exercises. It wasn't Rev. White but his assistant who insisted that I had walked the same path for fifty lifetimes and each one led down the same road. I was a teacher and a healer. Not wanting to previously acknowledge my path in favour of one of communication, I now wanted to embrace it. Perhaps I had been given this opportunity to be who I was supposed to be? If that was the case, the universe and myself were going to have words once this was all over.

I proceeded to meditate using the chakra balancing technique I use before any form of light work. I found it difficult to focus as my mind raced forward searching for guidance on how to proceed. I was finally able quiet my mind and concentrate on the white light that had started to fill every cell in my body. It was during that period of focus that I remembered my teenage years and more specifically, my discovery of candle magic.

The meditation ended. My chakras were balanced and I sat in silence. I let my mind take me back, back many years to my childhood bedroom. I was putting my spell candles away after an afternoon of practice when I stopped and set aside five candles. It could have been my imagination or it could have been the universe but following my own advice on the rule of first thought, it was important and I paid attention to the candles.

I was sure I still had some candles from a bout of spells I had done earlier that year. Selecting the colours I had seen during the meditation, I gathered the candles, essentials oils, a lighter, and my crystal ball. Not really knowing what I was doing, I just went with what felt right and well, just basically winged it.

Anointing the candles with orange oil, I informed the universe what role each candle played within the healing as I lit them. I did not think about it at the time but you would have thought the coloured candles would represent various chakras but this was not the case. Each candle seemed to represent either a physical part of Mickey or his psyche. With all five anointed, lit and in the hands of the universe, I sat back on the couch with my crystal ball.

Nothing happened. I really had no clue what I was doing. What was I thinking? I was no healer. I watched the candles burning as they danced and flickered with a strange synchronicity. Out of sheer desperation I selected a random meditation track on my computer, put on my headphones, closed my eyes and relaxed.

As I sank deeper into the meditation, I thought of Mickey. As I focused my thoughts, I pictured him sitting in the cold metal cage, scared, in pain and alone. The empathy I started to feel was like turning on a street light on a dark night and this brought the vision to life. I slipped in and out of my surroundings; lost in the meditation I felt a connection to Mickey build with each passing moment.

Out of nowhere and with no sense of how long I had actually been meditating, I found myself standing in front of the cage. I felt his relief as I opened the cage and carefully took him in my arms. His purr and look of pure love enveloped me as I held him to my chest. Our breathing as one, I felt a strange welling within me. It started at my feet and spread up through my entire body filling me with a sense of warmth and compassion. I was no longer thinking about what I should do, or how others healed, it was as though I had done it a thousand times.

Without a conscious decision, I exhaled and as I did I saw all the energy in the form of white light leave my body and enter Mickey. It happened very quickly, like opening a dam, and left me feeling empty and numb. This repeated four more times before I could no longer generate the sense of energy and started to lose my connection with Mickey.

I woke from my meditation and released my grasp on the crystal ball. I must have been applying a great deal of pressure as my hands began to regain sensation as I set the ball to my side. The five candleholders sat empty as all signs of what had transpired faded with the dissipating scent of burning orange oil. I am not sure how I felt about what had just happened, I still harbored the emotion I had felt but the vision was no longer foremost in my mind. I slowly rose and made my way to the kitchen. I was starving.

The next day I felt like crap. I was so sick; I could barely get off the couch. It was around lunchtime and the phone rang as the veterinary office number scrolled across the display. I didn't want to answer. At that moment anything was possible. The healing could have worked or he could have taken a turn for the worse. If I didn't answer, the only thing for certain was that there would be no change.

"Hello?" I said softly.

"Mr. Holgate?" A bubbly female voice sounded as my heart sank.

The rest of the call was a blur, but I remember thanking someone and making plans to pick up Mickey. Apparently his condition had completely reversed overnight. He was eating, his temperature was normal, and his tests were all clear. He was coming home.

Was this really me? Did I make this happen?

Mickey came home the next day but had it come at a cost? It had been two days since the healing and I had been sick ever since. The first day I could not even get off the sofa. As much as I had wanted to be there, I was not even able to pick him up. On the third day I started to feel more like myself and was able to move around the house and eat a little. It had not been a flu type of sickness, or anything I had experienced before, I was just sick. That's about as best as I can describe it.

Mickey was still himself and no worse for wear considering he almost succumbed to his illness. The one thing I did notice was that as soon as I was back on my feet, he did not leave my side for a week. If I sat on the sofa, he would squeeze himself in beside me. If I went to the bathroom, he would sit outside and wait for me. I guess this was his way of thanking me; I would like to think that anyway.

Talking to friends within my circle, they explained that rather than delivering white light and energy from the universe, I had used my own. This had left me drained and led to the subsequent sickness.

This is an important lesson for anyone who is considering healing. Practice using your body as a conduit for the universal energy; do not use your own. You may be strong, stronger than I am but until you begin the healing process you will never know how much energy will be required.

This distance healing happened on another occasion, but that time it also came with a remote diagnosis.

I was in the midst of Christmas shopping when I got a call from my friend and psychic mentor, Vanessa. It was just a call to catch up as it had been weeks since we last discussed my development, so the call was long overdue. Not long into the conversation I got a vision of my friend Pam that I found to be quite disturbing. I was still trying to process the vision when Vanessa asked if I was okay. I abruptly returned to the conversation but wasn't sure I should mention what I had seen. I was still new to these visions and had that underlying doubt that I could be imagining them.

I wanted to say something but what if I was wrong? I skirted around the vision, testing the water, always doubting that it was correct.

"How is Pat?" I asked sheepishly.

"She was fine the last time I saw her. Why do you ask?" Vanessa replied offering no indication that anything was wrong.

"I was just wondering," I sighed, half-convinced it was my imagination.

"Have you talked to her?" Vanessa asked in her regular chirpy way.

"No. Not for a while. Why?" My interest quickly turning to something shiny that caught my eye as I passed by an electronics store.

"I was just asking," she replied, but it felt like an interrogation.

"What's up with her?" I asked again, now focused on the conversation.

"Nothing," Vanessa answered abruptly.

"I know there is," I said, throwing caution to the wind.

"Have you talked to her?" Vanessa asked, genuinely interested in what I had to say.

"No, but I know," I replied.

"You know what?" Vanessa probed giving nothing away,

"It's-" I paused. I felt so much anxiety, I could barely get the words out. "It's in her chest area."

"Go on," Vanessa said as she encouraged me to explore my visions.

I was hoping I would receive some affirmation. Nothing. I am actually nervous again just recalling the moment. I took a deep breath and spit it all out.

"I see a lump in her breast. It is the right upper breast but is more a shadow than a solid lump but I can help."

I heard the words coming from my mouth, but I have no idea where they came from.

But I can help? What was I thinking? This is not a cat. This is a person, a real person and she is also my friend. I felt sick.

"Okay. You can't say anything," Vanessa's voice snapped me back into the present.

"Why?" I asked, excited that it wasn't just my imagination.

"She asked me not to say anything. Please, just don't say anything. She will tell you when she is ready," Vanessa replied with authority.

"Okay, I won't say anything. But I was right, wasn't I?" I asked half hoping I was right and at the same time wishing I was wrong.

Finally Vanessat responded, "Yes, you are right."

It was like a punch to the stomach, but could I really help? A month went by, thirty days of dwelling on the excitement that I was actually able to diagnose remotely, and the fear of what that could mean; then Pam called. I honestly do not recall the conversation, I was too nervous, but I do remember telling her that I had known for a month. Fighting the urge to commit myself to a healing that I was unsure would work; I eventually told her that I could help. That was a really big deal for me as it was an acceptance for myself, of my own ability. Score one for my subconscious mind. As I hung up the phone, the realization dawned on me, I not only now owned that statement, but also the expectation. Could I really do it?

A few days later, Pat dropped in and left me with a quartz wand and a feather. These items resonated with her so she asked that I use them as part of the healing process. I agreed even though I had not used anything other than my crystal ball, and to be honest, it really was the least of my concerns.

So, now we waited. I was not sure when it was going to happen, it just would. I think some of the delay was my own doubt, the rest was the universe. Maybe it sensed something?

The day arrived. It was just after nine on a Wednesday evening and I was given the green light. I turned off the TV and proceeded to do my chakra balancing. This was very difficult as my mind kept wondering about the healing. Balancing complete, I had to select my candles but only three came to mind this time. I am not sure why I needed fewer candles than I did for Mickey, but mine is not to question, I left that to my rule of second thought. Candles in hand, I anointed them with lavender oil. I should say that just like the candles, the oils were also shown to me, lavender being the one of preference for this healing. As I lit the candles I took a moment to address the universe.

"Dude, okay. If this works and I mean really works, I won't ever doubt you again. I swear, I will believe in all this."

I am not sure I even believed the words myself but I felt better having said them. It almost gave me that glimpse of exoneration if things didn't go to plan. I know, the self-belief has to be there, but this was not like asking for a cup of coffee, I am sure the universe understood. As it turned out, I have since had the same conversation over a dozen times as the universe and I have an understanding. I am neurotic while the universe demonstrates endless patience with me. It seems to work.

I again sat with my crystal ball cradled in my lap while the quartz wand and feather were placed either side of me. The healing followed the same course as it had when I worked with Mickey, however, with the difference being that I only felt the energy three times. Looking back, it actually took me a while to connect these to the number of candles selected; I never said I was quick on the uptake.

The next day I was sick again, but that time it only lasted for one day. I never told anyone especially Pat that I had done the healing, and if I am truly honest, I think that was just in case it didn't work. The following week a visit to see the people in white coats confirmed that the mass had indeed gone and has not returned to this day.

Was it me or just a coincidence? Don't get me wrong, I believe in what I do and I believe in the process. I sometimes still find it hard to believe in the results but as I said, the universe and I, we have an understanding.

What did I learn from this?

Well for one, when you take a course at Lily Dale or anywhere else, you should pay attention. You are there for a reason whether you understand that at the time or not.

I am not sure how my method measures up to everyone else's but it was the one that came naturally. Under no preconception, I just let it come to me and believed in it enough to make it work. Don't get too caught up in how other people do what they do, concentrate more on you and what resonates with your energy. Remember, we don't heal anyone, they heal themselves. We offer them the energy and the possibility at which time it is their own journey. Some journeys will still come to an end. That's okay. All journeys come to an end. We are just here to provide a choice but in the end, that choice is not yours to make.

Throat Chakra
Vishuddha

COMMUNICATION

Vishuddha is depicted as a silver crescent within a white circle with sixteen light or pale blue or turquoise petals.

My Life as a GPS

My life is a GPS is quite a strange statement but stay with me and let me explain.

To set the mood, I had been married forever. Okay, slight exaggeration. It felt like forever, but in reality, it was eight years. We were driving back from a weekend event where we had attended a ghost conference when that idea came to mind.

We are creatures of habit; there is no denying that. We also tend to hold onto things and situations far longer than we probably should. In this particular example, I am using relationships though this logic could be applied to many situations.

Why do we stay in relationships longer than we should?

In my case it bore from fear of what this represented, DIVORCE. In my family I had seen almost every couple go through a divorce and witnessed the subsequent damage left in the emotional and often physical wake. As a youngster I had witnessed this first hand and had grown up with the effect it had on my family and how after all these years, it was still a delicate subject to broach.

In my mind, if I could avoid a divorce, then it would all be okay and I would not follow along the same paths. In the end a lack of communication and opposing growth led to the inevitable split.

Many people use GPS devices as they are often a standard option in today's vehicles. Other people use portable comparable options, but they all do the same job, identify and lead us along our chosen journey.

For many of us, the use of such devices is quite a recent exercise, but how long have our lives displayed similar traits to those of our humble GPS?

In life, we have a starting point that is typically our birth and an ending destination that could either be our final moment on this earth or the discovery of our life's goal purpose. It could also be anything in between, but for this example we will just assume it's one of those we just mentioned. The points of interest along the way may change as life offers up options and choices, but as the GPS can help you locate the closest restaurant; our life's GPS does exactly the same job for our life's path.

As we set out on our life's journey, the GPS is relatively simple. It has very few places of interest and is generally set by our parents. Our route mirrors theirs in many ways as we avoid the highways of stress and worry often traveled by them. Our journey, for the most part, is one of discovery; we observe our surroundings as we pass them by learning as we go. Some of us may have early detours that take us off the route programmed by our parents, but for the rest of us we continue our journey with an innocent oblivion.

As we grow older our paths may offer alternative routes through the people we meet and through the opportunities presented to us. Though the destination remains the same, our route is adjusted through the choices we make. As we grow and the choices in our lives become centered more about our own needs and wants as opposed to those chosen on our behalf by our parents.' The points of interest on our journey increase in both quantity and variety as we open our lives to more possibilities. Now our life's GPS pertains to all aspects of our lives but in order to keep this example short and to the point, let's look at how this works with relationships.

You enter into a new relationship and everything is great. Your starting location is set and a possible destination is entered. There are always many potential exit points in any relationship and the number of points of interest can have a significant impact on the final destination.

So off you go, a full tank of gas that you both paid for, your drinks of choice neatly seated in the cup holders, the GPS set, life could not be better. The road is smooth, the traffic hardly noticeable as you enjoy quaint roadside stops along the way. It almost feels like this trip has been planned specifically as all the points of interest seem to appeal to you both.

The weather starts to turn a little grey as spots of rain threaten to spoil the roadside stops. You don't seem to mind the rain too much but you start to notice that the last few you stops you passed did not really appeal to you as much as the earlier ones did. You stop for gas but you don't have cash on hand. It's okay, you can get it at the next stop.

The journey continues but you both seem content to sit in silence for long periods as you pass stops without interest. You stop again for gas but it's raining quite heavily now and your jacket is in the trunk along with your wallet. You will get it next time. With the gas paid for again by your partner, you continue along the road but this time the silence following the transaction is accompanied by a sense of resentment.

You pass a small antique shop that seems to have nothing but junk on the front porch and you continue pass despite the request to stop by your partner. Apparently the rusty remains of a forty-year-old watering can holds a great amount of appeal to everyone but you. Shortly afterwards a quaint bookstore catches your attention. The thought of discovering a lost first edition at a great price is too much for you to pass up on. You pull in and are greeted with a sullen response from your partner and enjoy the bookstore alone. Returning to the car you receive little to no enthusiasm as you display your triumphant find. How can you be the only one excited about it?

You no longer stop at any of the points of interest along the route, they don't hold the same appeal to you as a couple any longer so stopping at none of them seems the only fair approach.

The first natural exit rapidly approaches. The GPS indicates the turn but you are distracted because of the lack of unity you seem to be experiencing. As you pass the exit, you enter a period of arguments and allegations all stemming around the ability to read a damn road sign. The arguments don't last long as the GPS re-calculates the route and sets the next natural exit. You continue along the highway with the patterns repeating themselves. The periods of calm following a missed exit seem to last longer and are more frequent as the natural exits come more frequently as the destination point edges closer. The recalculations and arguments are often more intense for finding an alternative route the closer you get to the end of the journey becomes increasingly more difficult. There are simply less options with some even requiring a U-turn to get back on the right route.

Just like relationships, we too face natural exits and often the decision to get off the highway is overlooked for fear of a new road. What if the GPS didn't have this road loaded? Or there were no stores or gas stations? These are all valid concerns, but if we continue along routes that are simply not working for us we will only be allowed to progress down them until we are forced to make an exit. By the time we reach that point in the destination we could be faced with a reduced number of roads. We may only have a left or right option with neither offering the route we would have chosen if we had taken the chance to exit earlier. Should we continue along the road simply because we know what to expect and where the gas stations are?

As I mentioned earlier, we are creatures of habit; there is no denying that. We also tend to hold onto things and situations far longer than we probably should.

So why should we take a chance on a new route?

"Because you have been there and know where it begins and where it ends."

What did I learn from this?

Though not strictly related to a GPS, the following illustrates the often confusing and frustrating confrontations we often face within relationships. In all reality, it is just a selfish indulgence on my part. The following is a parody on Monty Python's *Dead Parrot Sketch*.

Dingle-ding, the office bell sounds as you enter the universe's Offices for Relationships.

"Morning."
"Good morning, sir. How can I help you?"
"I would like to return this relationship please."
"Return the relationship sir?"
"Yes. I would like to return this relationship."
"Well, how long have you had it my good man?"
"Eight years, and I prefer 'sir' if you don't mind."
"Sorry, sir, of course, and how can I help you this morning?"
"It's this relationship. It's boring."
"Yes of course sir, one boring relationship. Well how long have you had it?"
"Eight years."
"Eight years eh? Well, we normally only allow two years for returns."
"But I didn't need to return it after two years."

"Why not, sir?"

"Because it wasn't boring then."

"It wasn't boring, sir?"

"No, it wasn't boring."

"Well, my old cock sparrow, it's not normally my policy to accept returns after two years."

"Cock Sparrow? What the hell is that?"

"What is what, sir?"

"The cock thing."

"I am not really comfortable discussing your cock, sir."

"It was you who said cock first. 'My cock sparrow,' you said."

"You have a sparrow? I thought you said it was a relationship, sir."

"IT IS a relationship."

"Then why did you say you had a sparrow, sir?"

"I didn't. YOU did."

"I did, sir?"

"Yes, you did."

"Why would I ask about your sparrow, sir? This is the Office of Relationships."

'Okay, look, I have a relationship. It's boring. I have had it eight years and I would like to return it PLEASE. No cocks, no sparrows, just this damn relationship, okay?"

"Well since you put it like that my old mucker, let's take a look shall we?"

"Mucker?"

"Mucker what sir?"

"You said Mucker, not me."

"Not you sir?"

"Not...what? Look this is just getting stupid now."

"Very good, sir"

"Very good what?"

"Your stupidity, sir."

"What? No...I meant this is stupid, not me."

"Sorry sir, of course, sir...So, what exactly is stupid here?"

"Okay, I have had enough. Is there anyone else I can talk to?"

"Regarding what, sir?"

"This relationship!!!!!"

"This one here, sir?"

"YES!! This one here."

"Well it's not very active, is it sir?"

"That's because it's boring. Didn't we already establish this?"

"Establish what, sir?"

"That it's boring."

"What's boring?"

"Are you even listening to me?"

"Yes, sir. It's a lovely day, sir."

"It's a what?"

"The day, sir. It's quite lovely."

I let out a sigh.

"Sir?"

"Listen, dog fart, I am just about done with you. I will take this relationship and stick it up your..."

"Okay. Okay sir. Sorry, let's not go there, Sir. So, this relationship here?"

"Yes?"

"And what is wrong with it, sir?"

"It'ssssssssss boring."

"Boring, eh. Are you sure, sir?"

"I'm sure."

"It looks okay to me, sir."

"Trust me, it's boring."

"Sir, relationships are sometimes boring for periods of time for no apparent reason. It's really quite the phenomenon."

"Periods of time, periods of time; it's been over four years since it showed any signs of life."

"May I look at the relationship, sir?"

"By all means."

"It's a little crusty around the edges, sir."

"Crusty around the edges, what the hell is that supposed to mean?"

"Ha. That's what she said, sir."

"What!!?"

"Sorry, sir. Just a little relationship humour, sir."

"Seriously. I want to talk to someone else."

"Regarding what, sir?"

"This relationship."

"Why, what's wrong with it?"

"It's boring!!!"

"Well, assuming it is boring, sir..."

"It is."

"How did it become bored, sir?"

"Do I look like an expert on relationships?"

"Apparently not, sir?"

"What is that supposed to mean?"

"Nothing at all, sir."

"Did it tell you to say that?"

"Say what sir?"

"That I don't know anything about relationships."

"You don't, sir?"

"Don't what?"

"You don't know anything about relationships, sir."

"Who are you to say that? You don't even know me."

"Why you did, sir."

"Okay, you are really starting to annoy me now."

"Bit of a temper, sir?"

"What?"

"I see you have a bit of a temper, sir."

"Only when it comes to this damn relationship!!!"

"What relationship, sir?"

As I mentioned, I think this was more for me than any actual bearing on my spiritual journey other than it certainly raised my spirits while I wrote it.

Is There Anybody There?

I f you are uncomfortable with the sheer thought of Ouija boards, you should skip this section. Seriously, put the book down now, before it's too late, for you can never come back from whence you came. Do I hear something behind you? Too late, you are now possessed.

Are you still with us?

Ouija boards get a bad rap, but do they really deserve it? Just the name, Ouija conjures thoughts of demons leaping out of the board spurting words from ancient rituals. We either know someone who has a story regarding an otherworldly experience, or we can recount one of our own. Either way they have been tarred, feathered, and cast out with distain. I am not going to try and convince anyone to rush out and buy one, but let's discuss our old friend Ouija for a while.

Ouija boards or similar forms of divination have been used for thousands of years. We can track their lineage all the way back to ancient

Greece where they were used as a tool of sight rather than one of fear. Around 540 B.C. the philosopher Pythagoras used what was described as a talking table. Fixed atop wheels, he would decipher messages for the waiting crowds who were amazed at this ability. Closer to home, some North American Indians were also known to have used a spirit board but they called it a *Squdilac*.

During the Second World War, the sales of Ouija boards hit an all-time high. As the soldiers fought overseas, loved ones used the boards to communicate with the other side. Contrary to how we use them today, no news was definitely good news as a connection from the other side could confirm their worst fears.

Consider this; over the past two thousand years millions upon millions of people have used Ouija boards in some form on a daily basis. Given the reputation that surrounds them, wouldn't you expect there to be reams of manuscripts depicting scenes of possession? So why isn't there?

Where did all this fear come from?

We don't hear stories of terror or possessions from people performing the "Bloody Mary" ritual, so why do we throw out the ability to rationalize when it comes to Ouija boards?

Many people consider mirrors as a portal to the other side, yet some people have a hard time passing one by without stopping to look at themselves. Typically a Ouija board is a pressed cardboard product with little to no conductive properties, they are far less common than a mirror, share a shelf in the toy stores with *Candy Land* and some even glow in the dark.

In 1973, a movie was released which would change perceptions forever. Dubbed as one of the most terrifying movies ever made, the reverberations are still felt today. The movie was, of course, *The Exorcist*, and could be considered as the single most important piece of media to provide weight against the use of Ouija boards.

During the making of the movie, technical advisor Father John J. Nicola urged the studio not to release the movie in fear of the potential hysteria the movie could command. Of course they didn't listen, the movie was released, hysteria ensued and more Ouija boards were disposed of following the release of the movie than at any other time.

For the majority of us, our first exposure to a Ouija board occurred as a teen while we were at a party or with a bunch of friends. These environments lend themselves to suggestion and often produce some scary results. How much of it is actually demonic presence and how much is a result born from our expectations?

"The glass flew off the table scattering the rough-cut pieces of paper we used for the letters around the room."

How many of us have similar stories? I have literally heard hundreds of variations. I am not insinuating that this never happens; I am sure some people do share authentic activity, but other than the wild stories of possession found on social media sites, how many people over the thousands of years of use have actually been possessed? Food for thought, indeed.

Before we talk about the reason why you should not use a Ouija board, let me leave you with a few last thoughts.

I have organized numerous Ouija board events where groups of people have used many boards with no adverse effects. As for the participants, when asked what messages they received, not many could actually recount anything in detail, but remembered more the overall experience. For the most part, we dismissed what we received as light conjecture or dare I even say it, entertainment. In the event that an actual connection to a spirit is achieved, we would have to put this information into some sort of perspective. Spirits often carry over characteristics they demonstrated while they were amongst us.

Would you take the advice of a total stranger you bump into on the street? So why do we take what we receive from the same people as the literal truth because the communication was received while using a Ouija board? A misinterpreted tarot reading has the potential to cause unspeakable damage yet we hold this form of divination in high regard. Why do we hold the messages we receive from the Ouija board accountable without question, while we so easily accept or dismiss others?

If you are feeling adventurous, look for some books written by Patience Worth. Patience was a spirit who through Pearl Lenore Curran wrote a number of books and poems. Using communication methods including Ouija boards, Pearl penned the words of Patience. These books are still available for purchase on Amazon and other bookseller sites.

Before you all throw this book down in anger, I do believe there are times the board should not be used. Contrary to what you have just read, I do subscribe to the view that Ouija boards can be very dangerous when used incorrectly and without precautions. Our intention plays a huge role in the light work we carry out but the same could be said for the times we dabble with avenues of the paranormal, Ouija being one of them. It's a morbid curiosity we have that first drives us to try the board and often keeps us coming back for more. As with any mode of spirit communication, the weak of mind or spirit can often be influenced by such use. I would never condone or encourage minors to use Ouija boards, nor would I allow anyone who suffers from mental illnesses or is under the influence to participate in an event.

I myself have experienced strange occurrences while using a Ouija board. Many moons ago I hosted regular séances at my house every Saturday night. Suffering from a lapse in creativity, these would come to be known as the Saturday Night Séances.

On one particular evening we had finished early due to a lack of spiritual activity. It was that or we had run out of Crown Royal whiskey, either way, only six of us remained. As we chatted about the decreasing size of whiskey bottles, we came to the realization as you do, that we had representatives of all four elements.

Some ancient Greek philosophers believed that the universe is composed of a mixture of four elements, Earth, Wind, Fire, and Water.

With four of our group representing each element, we wondered if having all the building blocks of the universe on the board would lead to better results. If you are interested in learning which element you are based on your birthdate, there are tools available on the Internet that will help you achieve this.

With Ouija boards always close to hand, we decided to put our theory to the test and attempt to jog some spiritual activity. The session started slowly with the customary round of "did you push that?" "No, did you?" before we ran into a pocket of activity. The planchette moved in a figure eight, then reversed before settling on random patterns. With interest peaking in the room, the planchette picked up speed as the movement became more erratic. The randomness of the patterns and letters had not revealed anything intelligible, though the sheer purpose of the movement was enough to hold our attention. Being paranormal investigators, we placed a digital recorder on the table. This act encouraged an insightful line of questioning that opened with,

"Is there anybody there?"

Okay in retrospect, it was not too insightful so let's just move on shall we? As we continued with our *traditional* line of questions the planchette grew increasingly more erratic and almost bounced off the board at one point. It was at that time we decided to take a break and reluctantly removed our fingers from the planchette.

As we slowly fell back into our prior seating arrangements, there was a mixed reaction to what had just happened. A couple displayed clear signs of excitement, but the resounding reaction was one of disappointment. There was no doubting the level of energy required to produce such activity, but the lack of real communication and the hint that maybe we were pushing it was enough to cast an air of doubt over the session.

I hit play on the digital recorder and tossed it back onto the board in the middle of the room and recovered my drink. I had grown bored of the conversation regarding the difference between a spirit moving the planchette and someone pushing it and focused on the comforting sound of white noise from the recorder's small speaker as I nursed the last of the pop. I heard the faint scraping sound generated by the planchette as it scoured the surface of the board, but there was little else to peak my attention. I heard the calls from the observers on the couch as they echoed the letters we received. The initial enthusiasm quickly gave way to indifference as the randomness became quite apparent. It was at that time our questions began.

"Is there anybody there?"

I heard my voice clearly through the speaker and wasn't really expecting anything in response; I definitely was not expecting to hear what followed.

"He's coming," a deep whispering voice announced.

Every ear in the room quit what it was doing and focused on that two-inch speaker in the middle of the coffee table. The discussion regarding who did or didn't push the planchette no longer seemed important. Who was coming?

Now, if any of you remember playing rock albums backwards and hearing hidden messages in them, then this will take you right back to the eighties. The voice that came from the speaker had an eerie awkward tone as you would expect from backward-spoken words. To be honest, if I never hear that voice again, I am good with that. It is almost like those photos or videos you force yourself to watch online, they can never be unseen. Like those, this voice could never be unheard. It was just plain spooky, even for our standards and continued for what seemed like an eternity, but in reality it was around five seconds. I reached for the recorder, hit stop, and tossed it back onto the board though the silence of the room offered no comfort.

"Whoa, what the...!" I exclaimed, more for myself but directed at everyone else in the room. I was actually shaken; it really was one of those defining moments of belief that there really might be things out there that go bump in the night.

The room was silent as we all blankly looked at each other. Time stood still as *the voice* found sanctuary in the dark corners of the room. This brief respite did not last as our morbid curiosities turned the stunned silence into a unified thirst for more.

I leaped up to grab the recorder before someone else beat me to it. Plugging in the USB cable I proceeded to download the audio to my computer and we waited for what seemed like an age. The software downloaded in real time so the captured audio was reflected visually in the equalizer that filled the top half of the monitor. The red peaks indicating either voice or loud noises provided encouragement as we bore witness to the capture of this demon-like voice.

Finally, it was imported. I powered up the stereo speakers, clicked play and you could have heard a pin drop. The hiss from the speakers barely masked the sound of the planchette or the whispers that were inaudible when we listened through the small digital recorders speaker. The clink of a glass, the shift in the chair; we listened intently to the voices calling out the letters and the sound the planchette as it picked up speed. We waited for the voice.

"Is there anybody there?" I swear you could hear every heartbeat in that room as we all held our breaths.

"He'ssssss coming," a voice hissed.

Full body goose bumps, it sounded far more foreboding through the large speakers than it had through the small speaker on the recorder. We braced ourselves for what we really wanted to hear. Nothing. The backward spoken words had gone and were replaced with white noise and the sounds from the planchette. Analyzing the audio further produced nothing; the voice we had heard had really gone. We had either all imagined what we had heard or even more concerning, we heard it live.

As nervy as that experience was, it had no lasting effects and did not prevent any of us from using the board again on many occasions and we never again heard the voice.

I know what you are all going to say, we should not be drinking while using a Ouija board. I agree but we didn't really drink too much and we have all been doing it for many years. We were safe and nobody ever suffered from anything more than a few goose bumps and a temporary aversion to dark places.

Another stand-out moment happened just a couple of months ago as we investigated a local Mennonite church from the early eighteen hundreds. We had split up into small groups of five or six people and were rotating so we could investigate the church inside and out. We had scattered our equipment and placed a Ouija board on the table that was often used as an altar during Sunday mass. There was no malice in our decision to use the table; we simply had no other options other than using the damp floor.

The evening passed slowly and uneventfully, other than a couple of lights observed using the thermal imaging unit. I guess out of boredom, a couple of the investigators placed a K2 meter on the Ouija board as it sat atop the altar. A K2 meter is a device we use to test electromagnetic fields with the idea that spirits will affect them, which is then communicated through a series of coloured LEDs on the device.

It immediately sprung to life with a dazzling light show as the green and red LEDs erupted. It didn't take long for the whole group to huddle around the altar, all thoughts of fear regarding the Ouija board replaced again with the same curiosity that brought us to the church in the first place. In the spirit of being somewhat scientific, two other K2 meters were placed on the board and immediately confirmed the activity. We now had three units filling the walls of the church with the LED light of activity.

Was this proof of a spectral presence? Probably not, so we started to really put it to the test. We removed the board from the altar and still they lit up. In the event that there were hidden cables in the floor, we carried the board with the meters to the other side of the church. Still they lit up. We removed the meters from the board which caused them to immediately cease all activity. We then placed them back on the board and again they sprung to life. It wasn't the altar after all, it was the board itself. This activity lasted for a good ten minutes before it tapered off. We even had some success controlling the intensity of the lights by simply asking them to change.

What can we take from this?

The use of the Ouija board is a personal choice. They have been used far longer than most people are aware of and do control a modicum of fear and apprehension. Some people will not use them without white light or an opening prayer where some people jump straight in and use them with willful neglect.

It's a personal choice but the one thing that really should be common across all approaches is the clarity of the intention and the emotion associated with it. If your intention is to draw negative entities, then the odds are that you will indeed succeed though you may not always realize it. If you enter with love and of pure intention then you should be able to enjoy your experience, though there are some exceptions to the rule as there are with all forms of communication and divination. Use your common sense, do not accept everything you receive as the gospel truth, keep your wits about you and surround yourself with a trusted group who has similar intention.

There are countless books on the subject but they are pretty subjective for the most part. Some condone them while others condemn the use of them with zeal. Many people are under the belief that we have skills that lay dormant within us. Long forgotten and passed over as we engross ourselves in a materialistic world, they await our awakening.

Perhaps this form of communication was one of them? Is it possible that Pythagoras knew something we don't? After all, I hear he was quite an intelligent chap.

The next time opportunity presents itself, give it a go, you might surprise yourself and even enjoy it.

OUIJA
Opening Protection Prayer

You can use any prayer for protection or white light, but here is one that was written specifically for this book.

We call upon spirit and the archangels to bring light to this session,
Protect us from all evils and provide only truths for this; our lesson.
Cast your net of light preventing darkness from entering this space,
And protect us all from now hence forth with purity and grace.

He Slimed Me

I never really went on many ghost hunts when I lived in the U.K. Why would I hunt for them when they are always around us? At any rate, that was my view at the time. The concept of packing up thousands of dollars' worth of equipment, driving for hours, depriving myself of sleep in order to spend three days listening to the recorded audio of the investigation I actually attended, seemed like a colossal waste of time. Why would I do that? In the hope of capturing a cryptic sound loosely resembling an inaudible voice? I already knew that spirits were around us, whispering words of encouragement into our bereft ears, yet there I found myself, one-fifteen in the morning, two days without sleep, minus three inside, sitting on a rusty bunk on death row, really needing to pee, and it was awesome.

I took to paranormal investigations like a duck to water. A few fluffed feathers aside, I had managed to navigate the proverbial pond with the grace of a clumsy swan. Going overboard as I normally do, I have amassed quite the collection of equipment and gadgets, some of which I designed myself. I currently operate three paranormal groups with around two-thousand members. It is somewhat of a commitment.

So why would I spend all this time, energy and money on something I already knew was there?

When I have a good enough answer for you I will let you know, until then let's just say I continue to provide the opportunity for others to realize their paths. With the advent of paranormal shows on television, many people have developed quite the curiosity for the other side. Some people watch in the hope to someday participate in an investigation where others believe it is the devil's work, yet they continue to watch the shows. It is almost akin to the fascination with Howard Stern throughout the nineties. A vast number of people loved his shows and hung onto every word. On the flip side there were also those who hated what he stood for but listened more regularly in order to know what to complain about.

The paranormal shows seem to command a similar reaction as they become more prolific through the channels of reality TV. They expose concepts about the possibility of "the other side" to the general public and offer a darker option to the mainstream.

An assortment of enthusiasts often find their way to groups like the ones I run where we offer them the chance to participate in an investigation. By affording the curious an opportunity to see just what goes into an investigation without having to commit financially, groups can provide a platform towards the next step or just offer a one-time experience.

Some people stay the course and even end up forming their own groups. Others return to their lives, having dipped their toes into something they weren't ready to understand. For some, I see these investigations as a philosophical gateway drug. It is often the first introduction to things we cannot physically grasp, and can open spiritual doors as growing interest in psychic awareness triggers a new model of thought.

So other than providing a platform for others to embark on their own journeys, what do I get out of the investigations?

I am not sure any longer. Like most investigators, I would strive to be the first to capture un-refuted evidence of life after death. After many investigations and sleepless nights combing through mountains of media, I quickly lost the ability to focus for more than thirty seconds at any one time. For a research investigator that was quite the crutch given that the majority of time is spent rummaging through said materials. I still own the equipment and given that I have spent thousands of dollars and countless hours on developing the groups, I feel I owe it to myself to keep plugging on.

Don't get me wrong, it has its moments for sure, but at this point in time it feels like it is almost a social exercise more than a true investigation. In order to keep the group fresh and to offer a varied catalogue of events, I try to find subjects and locations that appeal to me and encourage the enthusiasm I once felt and hope that these choices appeal to everyone else in the group. Perhaps the enthusiasm will return; perhaps the new round of members who attend the events will provide the spark that ignites the passion I once had. We can only hope.

Do I have any pearls of wisdom to pass on?

Sure. Don't eat a bowl of Brussel sprouts before an investigation. It can lead to hours of amusement as disembodied scents are attributed to lost souls, but in the end the giggling always gives you away.

If you want to try some investigating and there are no groups close by, you can do it relatively cheaply. Purchase yourself a digital recorder; eBay has some great deals but look for one that has a USB output. Now the die-hard investigators will tell you that you should use a tape recorder, only record on one side and only use the tape once. Nonsense. You go right ahead and get the digital one with the USB output. It will save you countless hours and grey hairs while you wait to transfer the audio to your computer. It will also be far cheaper than buying tapes. Besides, who sells tapes any longer?

You are not doing this to prove anything to anyone but yourself, so make it is easy as possible and select the equipment that will help rather than hinder you. If having the collective authority that is the paranormal community accept your findings as proof, then by all means purchase all the recording equipment you think you need. I use Olympus digital recorders primarily, which start around forty dollars depending on the model. You will also need a good pair of headphones. I prefer the noise cancelling type, as they will help to isolate those sounds that may be voices from the background white nose. They are also great if you find yourself being nagged; there really is something to the sounds of silence.

You can use the headphones with the digital recorder but I would suggest you download the audio to a computer. For one, the audio playback is normally far superior to that of the digital recorder and second; you create a copy of the audio. You may have captured an amazing class A EVP only to press the delete button as you accidently lean on the recorder. It happens...so I am told.

Just to clarify, an EVP or Electronic Voice Phenomenon is a voice that has been captured on a recording device. The idea is that through the background noise of the magnetic tape or the white noise of the room itself, the spirit could use that to impart a voice. Your recording device is acting as a "spiritual vocal box" for want of a better term.

If you are comfortable with what you may uncover, by all means set up the recorder in your own house. I must warn you that I have a friend who spent three months in the same boxer shorts because his wife tried that in the laundry room and scared herself half to death with what she recorded. Looking back, perhaps this was just a clever ruse to get out of doing the laundry. So unless you have an inert aversion to doing the laundry, go right ahead. For the braver ones, try leaving the recorder next to the bed while you sleep. That's always fun. Not!

Once you have the audio, download it to your computer, you can break it down, filter out background noise, and discover your own EVP's. There are many pieces of software you can use for this but a free one I recommend is called "Audition" and comes with a filter to export to mp3. There you have it; you can now start your own group, but before you rush off, I feel Genesis 1:3 offers a stark reminder of one of a group's most fundamental piece of equipment, so don't forget your flashlight.

From tiny recorders mighty paranormal groups grow.

Just remember, you are not trying to convince everybody that ghosts exist, you only need to prove it to yourself, and the rest of the world will take care of itself.

Through the many investigations I have attended, a few of them stand out for different reasons. I will share a few experiences with you now. Nothing too scary, just enough to keep you awake tonight.

I am often asked about orbs and if I think they are real or not. It's actually quite a contentious subject with many opinions and beliefs, but as always I have my own views on them. For the most part, a great deal of what I have been shown in video and photographs can be attributed to dust, pollen, or other airborne particles including bugs. This is not to say that some of them might be something else. I have had first-hand experience to support such claims and do not dismiss them all out of hand without first asking myself a couple of questions.

Are they self-illuminating?
Do they show signs of intelligence?

There have been three occasions where I was able to answer "yes" to both questions. The first was at a Muskoka Inn located in Southern Ontario. It was an originally a postmaster home and served as the local post office before it became an Inn. Having run an investigation all night, we had set up in the dining room for a late night séance. Around half-way through I decided to go back upstairs to the room we had deemed as the lights on room simply because we left the lights on. We had set up the monitor for the infrared cameras placed around the Inn with one located in the adjacent bedroom. I settled in to watch but there was little activity around which was a little disappointing, that was until I looked at the camera located in the next bedroom.

The orbs were going crazy, and I say that with all due respect, but simply stating that it was erratic behavior really does not describe it. With the séance having come to its conclusion, other members of the group joined me and we all observed the activity together. It wasn't long before some of the members wished to sit among the orbs to see if their presence would have any impact on the activity.

One by one we each entered the room to take our turn to sit among the orbs. I can't remember who entered the room first but as soon as they did, the activity abruptly stopped. We took turns in the room; some sat on the bed, others danced around the room but each time the outcome was the same. The orb activity stopped as soon as anyone entered the room. On every occasion, upon the investigator leaving the room the activity returned in earnest.

During my time in the room, I jumped on the bed and slapped the carpet in front of the camera producing nothing, not even a little dust. As interesting as that activity was, when I got the DVR home and exported the video, everything went well right up to the time I started watching the orbs at which point the video was corrupt. The size of the file indicated the expected length of footage but I was never able to recover that hour of footage that we all witnessed.

The second time that orb activity really left a lasting impression on me was during an investigation at a small museum in Buffalo, and this time it was with my naked eye. Iron Island Museum was, and still is, a popular stop on the paranormal circuit.

Having started its life as a church, it then became a funeral home before opening its doors as a museum and remains so today. With such a checkered history, the residual energy you would expect to experience does not fail to deliver, leading to quite unexpected activities.

On this particular investigation I was alone in a small room that was once used for final preparations to a casket before it was placed for viewing within the adjacent chapel. A tall ladder extended up through a small opening in the ceiling and into a foreboding darkness. For anyone brave enough to peer through the hole, it opened up to the original cathedral ceiling of the church, still sporting the stained glass window.

As I approached the ladder, I felt quite uneasy about my decision to climb it, as an unusual feeling come over me. I instantly changed my mind and the ladder to the church ceiling remained unexplored by me on that particular occasion. The funny thing is, it eluded me on each visit, as there always seemed to be something that prevented me from taking a look through that dark hole in the ceiling. That time was no exception.

Turning to leave the room I immediately felt something or someone behind me. Now being the fearless paranormal investigator I wasn't, I refrained from looking behind me and quickly shuffled out of the room and into the chapel. To say I was a little panicked would in some part to undermine the idea that I was the fearless K2 wielding ghost hunter. In all honesty, I was crapping it.

As I approached the middle of the room I felt a notion of energy pass by my head, as whatever it was must have grown tired of my lack of physical reactions. I turned my head slightly out of pure instinct just in time to see a bright white orb pass by me and exit the room. I immediately stopped, not out of any form of curiosity but my legs had actually stopped working.

When I retell this story, I normally say it was a professional curiosity or a thirst for the truth and adventure. That's a lie. It was from shock. Collecting myself, the investigator in me began analyzing what had just happened and tried to rationalize it.

Were there any reflective surfaces in the room?

Was there a light source or window that a light could have come from?

No and No. Couple this with the feelings I had experienced in the room and immediately prior to seeing the orb, I came to the conclusion that I had indeed witnessed a paranormal activity, and once again my legs wouldn't work. I did actually see another orb later that night. I was meditating in a large wingback chair while facing a similar empty chair. As my meditation came to an end I noticed an orb appear around two feet above the chair. It gently descended and disappeared into the chair but that time my legs did indeed work as I hastened an enthusiastic retreat.

The most recent activity that I find difficult to dismiss happened while participating in a Halloween dinner and séance event in 2013. Located in a well-known building for paranormal activity in Fort Erie, The Dollhouse Museum, as it is known, sits on the Niagara River just minutes from the bloodiest soil in Canada. The War of Eighteen-Twelve left behind many relics, the most macabre of which are fallen soldiers who are still uncovered to this day during garden remodels or planned excavations. Birdie Hall, its official name, sits minutes from the Old Fort and it was heavily involved in the Underground Railroad.

The event was underway and our guests were all seated on the main floor enjoying the meal we had catered for the evening. We placed a Go Pro camera in the hidden basement to see if we could capture anything while everyone was on the main floor.

That particular section of the basement was located behind a hinged set of shelves and had once concealed the tunnel that led from the banks of the Niagara River to the house. The tunnel had been used as part of the Underground Railroad and has its own history of suffering and deaths within its dark damp passage. We left the camera recording for the remainder of the event but upon inspecting the video we discovered that we only had around seventeen minutes of video. That was odd considering we should have captured well over five hours of footage.

Upon first glance the video seemed stark of any sort of activity, that was until we looked a little closer. In no less than five areas of the basement we observed very strange orb activity. Orbs appeared, merged and moved so erratically that they closely mimicked the type of movement UFO witnesses have described. I have never seen such activity before this event, or since. The orbs showed clear signs of intelligence,

What kindled further interest was the fact that no flash or direct light source was used during the recording. In fact, a single low wattage bulb provided the only source of illumination. In the basement we also ruled out a breeze as we were situated below ground in the basement with no external entrances or windows. The staircase to the hidden basement was accessed through a larger adjacent room that was also locked at the top of the stairs. This activity has been posted on to our YouTube and Facebook pages with both links provided on the references page of this book.

So what did I learn about orbs and investigating in general?

It is important to remember why you are going to all the trouble to find evidence of life beyond ours. I say trouble as it often comes with a price tag requiring you to travel long distances and flourish under conditions you would normally avoid. You need to be content that you will not prove anything to the world; it's all about proving it to yourself. What you find is also unique to you. What I took from the experience with the orbs will not the same experience that it will be for you. It will mean something different to everyone so don't get despondent if other people just don't get it. They don't have to, only you do.

You may also get wrapped up in the equipment, especially if you watch any of the shows on TV and feel you need to own the same in order to see and experience what they do. The first thing to remember here is that it's TV. I shouldn't really need to elaborate on that but it's driven by ratings, use your common sense.

If you are a sensitive then perhaps try investigating with a group who has some psychic investigators and ask to work with one of them. You already come with all the equipment you need, but if you feel inclined to rush out and buy some gadgets, start with a digital recorder. Have a look on eBay for a decent digital recorder with USB out, and a pair of good headphones, preferable the noise cancelling ones and download an audio analyzing software for your computer. You can do all this for less than a hundred dollars, less than fifty if you really spend some time looking for the bargains.

Above all trust your gut feelings and don't second-guess yourself, rule of first thought.

Inspector Gadget

I have to build what?

Though not technically spiritual, the paranormal investigations I have organized and participated in have certainly contributed to my spiritual journey. The equipment we used makes up a large part of that and thus warrants an honorable mention.

My fascination with the paranormal or more specifically, the occult began at a very early age. I would be remiss not to attribute part of this fascination to my locale as I was born and raised in and around 'witch country,' but I was also gifted with an extremely active imagination that played its own role. When I was provided the means and reason to continue my journey into the dark corners of life while living in North America, I jumped at opportunity.

I was a couple of years into my Canadian paranormal adventure when I had an urge. No, it wasn't an urge like that, though it was quite strange and relentless. To those people around me who didn't really understand or condone my fascinations, this urge seemed almost disturbing in its manner.

So what was this urge? I hear you ask.

I had an overwhelming compulsion to design and create strange investigative devices. Now these were not just the run of the mill recording devices, some of the ideas I was received included some real wacky concepts. I distinctly remember the morning for one of them. It was a Saturday and I awoke on the basement couch having fallen asleep watching a Red Dwarf re-run marathon the night before with a picture of what could only be described as a pipe bomb affixed in my mind. Now before the urge to make a call and report this activity dominates your thoughts, this pipe bomb was nothing explosive.

My initial impression of the idea was one of apprehension, but the image of a four-foot length of black pipe with a wire protruding from each end lent itself to quite the vision of coolness. I had to build it. Before I embarked on this new journey into my wackiness, I meditated in the hope that it would provide a more focused vision, allowing a glimpse of what my goals were, and if indeed there was an end game. I knew that I couldn't afford to bring all the ideas I had received to life, so if I understood the roles they played perhaps I could make an educated decision allowing at least a few of them to come into fruition.

I did not receive any clarification, though I think my thoughts were clouded by the image of the pipe bomb. This was all somewhat a leap of faith. Was this an opportunity to trust my better judgment and simply pop in the next Red Dwarf DVD or should I really do this?

What do you think I did?

What was the pipe bomb?

It was nothing like the name suggests despite the commonalities you would observe upon seeing the device for the first time. I think the driving force behind a lot of the ideas I had was to simplify our approach, or "go back to the basics" if you like.

In this modern world we seem to take all our accomplishments and attempt to devise methods to replicate them using electronics and microprocessors, but there was some pretty cool science behind our past accomplishments that we sometimes tend to overlook. This particular approach would see the use of elements such as carbon and germanium, even water and light to produce a communication device.

My idea was to create carbon and germanium based solutions, fill the pipe with them, add rubber caps on either end to seal the pipe, then pass sound through the liquid and record what we received. Sounds simple, but where would I get a microphone and speaker that would work in both carbon and germanium based liquid? The answer to this was a dolphin laboratory in Florida.

I would like it to go on record that no dolphins were hurt during the manufacturing of this device.

This particular laboratory specialized in the recording of sounds and songs for a wide array of marine life. I approached them for both a waterproof microphone and speaker in the hope that that they would not ask me what I wanted them for. Luckily for me they didn't, but that left me wondering if this was a common request they received. I am sure I would have asked had the roles been reversed.

So now I had a four-foot length of black pipe, two rubber endcaps, an underwater microphone and speaker but nothing to fill the pipe with. It would have been simple to purchase some carbon powder, add it to water and fill the pipe. That was too easy for me. I wanted to get carbon crystals from old handsets found in the telephones from the seventies and early eighties.

My logic seemed solid at the time given those carbon crystals had been used specifically for communications and may hold properties that would facilitate spirit communications. Let's just go with my logic here, after all this is not an exact science, there are no rules. I located a large batch of microphones from an electronic re-claimer in the UK and ordered a box containing around a hundred.

A few weeks later, a plain brown box arrived containing the microphones. This led to my next hurdle. How was I going to extract the carbon from them? They were sealed quite well as you would expect but luckily for me there was a tool designed specifically for that particular task. With a rather large flathead screwdriver in hand, brute force and ignorance worked remarkably well.

With the carbon extracted and ready to add to the water, I was faced with yet another hurdle. In order to project sound through the liquid, a microphone pre-amp was required. Finally, a mixer enabled me to split the audio between a powered speaker and digital recorder. Although rudimental in design, my masterpiece was complete. Despite the crude the manufacturing method, everything seemed to check out and was ready to go. With the investigation booked the inaugural use of the pipe bomb was just a few days away.

The Customs House, a notoriously haunted location in Hamilton, Ontario served as the launch pad for my new gem. The location had been known to drain batteries and other electronic devices in the past, but it had never met a pipe bomb.

Setting up the device in the main hall, the anticipation grew as we were all very optimistic. I think this was down more to my wild boasts than a confidence in the device itself. I placed the electronic components on the table and carefully placed the liquid-filled pipe in two makeshift cradles. Turning on the power, the speakers hissed into life. The bright green LED lights on the mixer created geometric patterns as the light navigated through the buttons and sliders before creating an eerie glow on the matt-black pipe. Just the pre-amp stood between live communication and me.

I plugged in the microphone and turned on the pre-amp. The hissing from the speakers increased, popped, and then...silence. The building so infamous in its effect on investigations and equipment had claimed yet another victim. Upon closer examination, the power to both the mixer and speaker seemed compromised, resulting in a premature end to the pipe bomb's first foray into the paranormal.

I never resurrected the pipe bomb though I do still have it. In pieces around the house I am not sure why I lost the desire to use it. Maybe it was the thought of having to buy a new mixer and speakers or perhaps the lesson lay within the process itself. I may try it again one day.

I had many ideas over a two-year spell and even hired electrical engineering students to build some of my crazy ideas. These ranged from communication through lasers and infrared light to ultraviolet microphones and mobile ITC. It was the latter that produced some of the most encouraging and unnerving evidence we have captured to date.

If you are familiar with the concept of Instrumental Transcommunication or ITC, you won't need any further explanation. For those of you who haven't a clue what I am rambling on about, ITC in its simplest form is the viewing and recording of looped video. You take a video camera and point it at a television. Press record on the video recorder and using the video out, plug a cable from the video recorder to the "video in" or "source" on the television. This creates a loop where you view what you are recording and record what you are viewing. Confused? Me too but a few minutes of research on the internet will help clarify the process. Honest.

The results can be quite remarkable with the screen exploding into plasma forms of swirling light and colour. If you take the recorded loop and analyze it frame-by-frame on a computer, you can sometimes see images of spirits who have passed. People who go through great pains to research ITC in detail may not agree with this simple explanation but it serves our purpose for this book.

I was fascinated with the concept but could not conceive of a realistic method to use ITC in the field of paranormal investigations. Rolling a thirty-inch television up and down a corridor while pointing a camera at the screen and asking "Is anybody there?" was not an ideal solution. Ignoring the sheer logistics of keeping the equipment at a fixed distance and avoid tripping over the trailing cables, imagine getting this lot up and down stairs.

Never one to be defeated, I pondered other approaches that would allow me to use ITC and then it came to me; I would use sound. For me it stood to reason that if we could capture occurrences while using video, sound should produce something too, shouldn't it?

Using my old bookshelf stereo and a couple of pocket radios, I purchased an FM transmitter and put my contraption to the test. First, I tuned the stereo to an empty frequency and then did the same with the FM transmitter. The stereo output was linked to the transmitter input, creating an audio loop. Another receiver was set up a distance away, also tuned into the same frequency. The output from this radio was fed into a digital recorder. The results were not as exciting as I had anticipated. In fact, they were downright boring, to the point that I did not try that method for a while. When I did attempt it once more, it was certainly worth the wait.

Replacing the shelf stereo with another pocket radio and purchasing a new battery-powered FM transmitter, I headed up to Bobcaygeon in southern Ontario to meet my friend Pam. The property we were visiting neighbored the Indian reservation and was known for Bigfoot and UFO sightings. I set up the ITC radio loop the same as I had on the previous attempt and placed the two looped radios in my jacket pockets along with the FM transmitter. I held the third radio along with the recorder at arm's length in order to create a wider loop. For approximately twenty minutes we recorded as we walked through the woods.

After we returned to the house, we pressed play on the recorder and placed it on the countertop as we made tea. At first there was only static but then, we heard it.

If you have seen the movie *Signs* and remember the scene with the baby monitor; well, that is exactly what we heard. A series of clicks; some elongated, some sharp and rapid, but certainly nothing we had heard before. It was pretty freaky and we wanted to record more but it was getting dark and we had a long drive back. In keeping with the spirit of science, we did stop briefly just outside Bobcaygeon to see what we could pick up but all we recorded was static.

All we really had at this point was a series of sounds. We had no real reference or notion as to what we had captured. That all changed two weeks later. There is a documentary called *Fastwalkers* that exposes the cover-ups and denials of alien contact over the years. One of the key figures who worked on the documentary was giving a lecture in Bobcaygeon. Coincidence? I think not...

It was a Sunday afternoon and I found myself sitting in a group of over fifty people who shared the same curiosity towards UFOs. As we listened to the lecture that in itself was interesting, we were really holding out for the crowning jewel. We were waiting to speak to a person who originated from the Mantis race. I know it sounds crazy, but you really needed to have participated in our recording not two weeks prior in order to accept any of it. If that recording had never happened, who knows? Perhaps I would have still been there but probably not.

The lecture over, the speaker made the anticipated phone call on his mobile. The woman on the other end of the phone seemed normal enough as she greeted him and everyone in the group. I was a little disappointed. I was expecting something out of a Sci-Fi movie or at the very least, a more unusual accent than my own. He then asked her to speak in Mantis and she sounded exactly like the recordings we had made.

Pam turned to me mouthing the words "WTF!" She always had a way of cutting through to the chase.

"I know," I mouthed back, wondering how I could add a profanity without it seeming out of place.

As the lecture came to its conclusion, we managed to get a few minutes with the speaker and recounted our story of the recordings. He didn't think we were crazy so that was a good start and he promised to pass on our contact information to the woman on the phone.

He was true to his word. Within a few weeks we received an email from the woman on the phone, who agreed to listen to our recording. We were convinced she was full of BS but I emailed her a portion of the recording anyway. Two days passed and I was sure we would never hear from her again, but to our surprise she responded. Now, we had not told anyone, even the speaker, where we had made the recordings or who owned the property. When I read the email, she talked about a conversation regarding a healer and the property she lived on. She then went on to say that we had only provided her part of the conversation and did we want the remaining translated. I was totally floored; she was completely accurate. How could she have known about any of it? I was so unnerved I never sent her the remainder of the recording.

The one piece of equipment that got away from me for many years was the Germanium Receptor. Designed by Thomas Edison as "the telephone to talk to the dead," it was used as part of the now infamous Scole Experiment. I was fascinated by the whole idea that physical mediumship was being used with amazing results. The receptor required almost one hundred percent pure germanium. For this I had to go to a lab I had found in Eastern Europe. The high resistance coils were quite difficult to locate as they are reminiscent of technology from a by-gone era and are no longer used to the same degree. After three years of scouring poorly created websites offering new and used electronic surplus, I am now the proud owner of the receptor and have acquired the remaining equipment to begin my own Scole Experiment. Stay tuned for more information. Perhaps I will one day write a book all about our experiences with physical mediumship.

So now what?

My drive to build wacky equipment has lessened over the years but I still have plans to build one or two items.

So why did I build so much?

Who knows? Perhaps it was a phase I had to go through in order to bring me to the point I find myself today. There are many influences within the paranormal circles that drive you to always have the latest and greatest equipment. When it really comes down to it, the best piece of equipment is you. There are no devices out there that can replace what you are capable of doing. Don't get me wrong. If you feel compelled to include some of the available equipment in your investigations or you even want to design your own, you should; you never know where it may lead you. The use of equipment kept me interested for a while and I am sure it attracts people every day to a field that is difficult at the best of times, so it certainly serves a purpose.

With millions of people around the world searching for evidence of paranormal activity and life after death, we still don't have that concrete evidence in the form of media. But do we really need it? We seem to spend so much time and money trying to prove this and that, but we never stop to think if we should.

Is there a reason we are still seeking that which has eluded us since we started asking questions regarding life after death?

Oh sure, there are some audio clips, photos, and even videos, but have we proven anything? Perhaps there is just no technology that can record our soul. Perhaps we are missing the most important question in all this; should we even be trying?

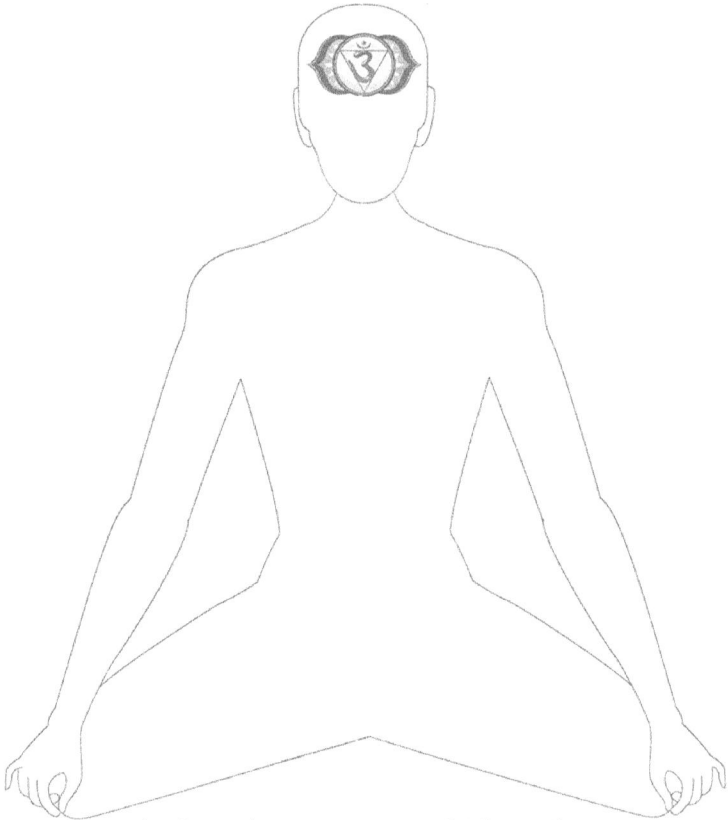

Third Eye Chakra
Ajna

INTUITION

Ajna is symbolized by a lotus with two petals, and corresponds to the colours violet, indigo or deep blue, though it is traditionally described as white.

Between the Lines

T his is just a short section that will touch upon aspects of life where you may experience change while opening yourself spiritually.

As my abilities grew so did some skills that were unexpected. One of which was the ability to see through the BS. It sounds like quite the boast and I guess on some level it is, but it really wasn't always the gift it promised to be.

Imagine a scenario.

You work for corporate Canada in a downtown office, representing the second largest publisher in the world. It's a Monday morning; the scent of Friday's Hawaiian shirt day still lingers in the hallways as you enter the boardroom. The large oval table seats twenty comfortably but keeping alive a habit formed from years of mischievous school days, you head for the back of the room. The meeting stutters to a lazy start with the presentation of last quarter's profits for both the European and U.S. markets.

As the third coffee of the morning begins to take effect, the anxiety knot of a psychic message starts to take shape in your chest. Hoping that the coffee is having a reaction to the previous evening's cider, you ignore the feeling and bring your attention back to the meeting. Budgets, the one subject guaranteed to put the room to sleep, claims its first victim. A wry smile breaks your deadpan stare as your gaze settles on one of the older managers entering the first phase of a fitful sleep. His face is a clear reflection of his dream which had obviously no bearing on the current subject given his slight twitching and drooling.

A twinge in your chest again focuses your attention to the anxiety as you start paying attention to your thoughts. Scanning the room you start to wonder who this message will be for and how do you go about delivering it? A sudden sound snaps back your attention as the sleeping manager's chin slips from his cupped hand, causing him to knee the underside of the table with enough force to tumble a plate of digestives by him. Laughing a little inside, you focus on the hum from conference phone in the middle of the table and wondered why you did not spot the biscuits sooner.

You zone out of the remainder of the meeting as you weigh the pros and cons of sitting closer to the biscuits next time. Though plain digestives would always take a back seat to the chocolate-covered alternative, any form of sugar is welcome this early into the work week. You are still contemplating whether you would rather be stranded on a desert island with dark or milk chocolate digestives when everyone begins to mill out of the door signaling the end of the meeting.

With the anxiety still present, you join your colleagues and slowly head back to your desk and towards what will be yet another week lost in perpetuity. Halfway back it suddenly dawns on you, you are not sure if you asked to do anything at the meeting. You decide to stop by the café on the way back to your desk. It's a great place to catch up on the latest gossip and you could always do with another coffee.

You are in luck as four of the managers who had attended the meeting are waiting for a member of the I.T. staff to remove a k-cup that seems to be wedged into place by a three-day old piece of pineapple.

Wondering if unbeknown to you, the fruit mishap was another of your office jokes gone wrong, you spark up a conversation with the only one you can actually stand to be in the same room with.

As you probe for a recap about the meeting and in particular anything that would require you to actually do something, the other three chirp in, triggering the anxiety in your chest to take on another form. We will cover anger and the urge to choke someone with a stale piece of pineapple another time, but for now we will deal with the current situation.

You listen to them as they talk at you rather than to you, as an image of a well-executed beating with a light sabre would seemingly go a long way to improving your office situation. As they continue their relentless jabber to the internal sound of "Manama na, do do, do do do", it then occurs to you, you hear what they are saying but receive what they really mean. If you are familiar with the TV show *True Blood* and the character Sookie Stackhouse, it is almost like that only you don't actually hear them or an internal dialogue; it is more a "knowing" of what they are really saying.

As you can imagine, this presents you with countless advantages but it also comes at a price. Along with the thoughts and feelings you receive during meetings and interactions with your peers, you also pick up on what is said and meant when you talk to your friends. Discovering you are not as popular as you thought you were, or worse, that you are even avoided when it comes to the game nights you initiated, leaves quite the sour taste in your mouth. Those with a weak volition may find this too much to handle. It really can rock your world for all the wrong reasons.

The good news is, this does not seem to happen all the time, but when it does, remember the rule of first thought and try not to rationalize what you receive, good or bad.

Now given that I have the ability to do this, it stands to reason that others must be able to also. How many times have I found myself in a conversation where I am the one being conservative with the truth while the other person sees through my words to the true meaning? It almost makes you want to stop and think about what you saying before you engage your mouth. The next time you find yourself in a difficult conversation or even chatting with a friend, just think about one thing. If they didn't hear what you were saying but instead what you really meant, would you still be having the same conversation?

Another thing I noticed while I worked at the same office was not as cut and dry. During one particular boring meeting with the president, I glanced out of the window. I noticed a dove perched on a wire that spanned the busy downtown road below. I was still wondering what a dove was doing there when I caught a glimpse of myself looking out of the window at dove, but I was the dove. I quickly snapped back into myself as the dove continued its journey to a nearby park, but the experience left me a little stunned.

Was it my imagination or did it really happen?

Was the meeting that mind-numbing that I took solace in the form of a dove to avoid listening to one more word? Perhaps this was the universe telling me that I should be looking for alternative employment.

This type of experience happened on numerous occasions and each time it was a bird that offered me the opportunity to see things from another perspective. It was not until I found myself on yet another long commute home that I focused my attention on a person sitting in one of the stationary vehicles around me. I was not even really aware of what I was doing. One minute I was day-dreaming and the next I was seeing the road from her view and could feel the frustrations of not only the lack of movement on the road but of the troubles at home the family was experiencing. I abruptly snapped back into myself in time to see the person I had just visited staring uncomfortably at me. Luckily for me it was a very attractive young lady so I simply smiled and returned my attention to my own line of vehicles extending out of sight ahead of me.

I never really explored what this was or if I could do more with it. It never really commanded my attention as I got wrapped up in the mundane trappings of my own surroundings.

A number of years later, I was able to connect to an eagle as we passed it on the highway, issuing a reminder that whatever skill this was had not forsaken me. As the bird came into view, its sheer presence was enough to capture my attention and cause my mind to return to that day I first connected with the dove. It was at that time I was able to feel the wind around me, the sense of the wooden fence below my feet and the blur of a red vehicle quickly passing as I stared out of the window in the direction of the bird.

I have still not explored this or researched what it really means. I am not suggesting that upon your spiritual development you are going to turn into every animal you come into contact with. After all, this could be quite disturbing if you found yourself at a dog park, given the customary canine greeting between consenting dogs.

This was just one example of something I noticed as I progressed through my spiritual lessons; your own journey could lead you down even more colourful paths.

Crown Chakra
Sahasrara

UNDERSTANDING

Sahasrara is symbolized by a lotus with one thousand violet petals; it is located either at the crown of the head or above the crown of the head.

Secret Garden

Creating a place of peace, comfort, and safety when on a spiritual path can be the difference between finding and living your path, or waiting for the next time round. Whether it is a physical location or one you create in your mind, we all need a place we can call our own and is always there for us. It is not always possible for us all to have that special place in our physical world, but the sky is the limit in our minds.

When I was very young I worked with many spells and psychic exercises. I was convinced that people were throwing psychic darts at me as I walked down the streets and don't get me started on psychic vampires. I felt safe in my bedroom, but as a young teen with a healthy imagination I set about creating a space that I could call my own and one where nobody could attack me; my own mind.

My introductions to meditation had been a little rocky as I had found the techniques I had been shown to be stuffy and difficult for me to commit to. Just as I had done with my spell work, it did not take long for me to develop my own approach. Having an affinity towards all things druid-like, I set out to construct a magical tower in my mind.

This tower sat amidst a large impenetrable forest, had one entrance and a single window located in the solitary room at the top of the tower. Before you ask, my preference in literature has always been that of the realms of fantasy so it came as no surprise to myself that the tower was a combination of Sauron's tower and something Macros the Black would have called home. Both these magicians play prominent roles in two series of fantasy books that I have read many times.

Just picture a very tall stone tower rising to a slate-clad coned roof. A solid oak wooden door guards the entrance to the interior spiral stone steps leading to a single room at the top of the tower. You know, thinking about it now, I never once recall having to walk up all those stairs.

Every time I visited my tower, which was most days, my vision of the tower grew in strength. I reinforced every aspect of the tower with each visit until it became so familiar that it really didn't take any effort at all to bring the vision to life within my mind. In no time, all I had to do was close my eyes and I was there. It was as vivid as any lucid dream. After a while I added items to my room like a bookcase, altar, and a large chair and desk to sit at. I even had a firedrake at one time but the damn thing flew out of the window and never came back. Just a quick note, if you thinking of creating your own tower, put glass in the window.

Over the two years that I used the tower I was aware of many changes. The moss that grew at the base of the tower steadily eked an existence between the large footstones. The ivy that was originally less than knee-high now stretched all the way to the top of the tower providing a home for small birds and spiders.

Why were there so many spiders?

Even the chair at the desk seemed to grow more comfortable the more I sat in it. I never took any books with me, but the bookcase was nearly full as I would often find books on my desk or left outside at the door. These were books that seemed to mirror my studies in the physical world. In short, my tower was a living environment that became as real to me as any place in the world around me.

I cannot really pinpoint the time I stopped visiting my tower but I feel it was a gradual transition. As I grew older, my spell work tended to take more of a back seat to my teenage adventures so the need for the tower waned along with activities. It was not until I started meditating later in life that I felt a need for a safe place once again. You would think that I would just pick up where I left off in my tower but this was not the case. As I thought of a safe place, I found myself in a small forest. My very own secret garden.

I refer to the forest as a secret garden. This is part due to the confinements I feel when I am there though no walls are present and it just feels like a garden. Unlike the tower, there was no sense of solitude though I have never met anyone in my garden who wasn't invited. I am not sure how large the garden is as I have never reached the edge. Each time I explore, I reach a point where the path is masked by a cold fog that prevents my progress. I have tried on many occasions but I always get turned around and find myself back in the garden. There must be a reason I cannot get past the fog, and I am now at peace with that.

The first time I visited the forest; there was a single path that led through a small stream to a tree-lined clearing roughly a hundred feet in diameter. A large trunk sat over a deep bowl that had formed in the middle of the clearing providing a perfect place to contemplate. When I visit to meditate I often sit on the log as there are fewer distractions due to lack of the animals and insects. Things never really change much in the clearing, though with it being open to the elements, it can lead to various states of mind during the meditations. On one occasion it even snowed and although it never really felt cold, it was still an unusual sensation while meditating.

Unlike the clearing, the forest is in perpetual transition and seems to respond to elements within my physical life. When I cross paths with animals they tend to be unaware as to my presence but still offer a sense of communication simply by being there. All interactions within the forest, no matter how trivial, seem have an influence on my experience. I have planted flowers and herbs and on my return they have grown, withered or simply done nothing at all. Rarely do I return to witness no changes have taken place.

Over the years the forest has expanded, allowing me to enjoy a multitude of individual and group spiritual activities. Some of these remain and became a permanent fixture while others provided a temporary platform to interact with my spiritual psyche on a "need to" basis. The forest seems to know what I need and provides accordingly. An old wishing well provided the basis for Law of Attraction exercises while an open-raised Dias allowed for group healings. These were just a few of the elements that mysteriously appeared during a time that reflected a need within my life.

I often hear the chants of monks from the path though their presence eludes me. I do sense the energy they generate, as it remains long after they have left the healing area and I often build upon this residual energy when performing my own healings. I have even conducted group healings within a meditation. This is almost like entering a meditative state while within a group meditation setting or experiencing a dream within a dream with the difference being we all entered the meditation sharing the intention and vision.

Everyone should have a quiet safe place to visit and with that in mind, we will begin the task of creating your own secret garden today.

In order to create your own safe place, you need to find a quiet area where you won't be disturbed. Ideally this would be done during a meditation session or when you go to bed. If you have a partner who fidgets, snores or worse, shares the by-product of their digestive process, you might be best doing this while you are meditating; alone and odor-free, if you know what I mean.

It may help to read part of this passage then stop to visualize it. Or if you are feeling confident, you can memorize this section so you don't have to stop. If you really feel inclined, you could record yourself reading this chapter and then play it back as part of your meditation.

When it comes to creating your own space, there is no right or wrong way, just your way.

You can use this exercise to create any type of location if the garden or forest doesn't appeal to you. Perhaps you want to build your own tower. The main thing is to create your own space, but remember, if you build a tower, make sure you have allocated the budget to cover glass for the window.

So let's begin. Perform your regular meditation in order to quiet your mind and raise your vibration. Remove your footwear and socks; you need to be in bare feet for this. From a seated position, get comfortable with your feet flat on the ground. Close your eyes and feel the chair you are sitting in. Be aware of how it feels beneath you; take notice of the temperature and the sensation of the material on your skin. Picture yourself settling into the chair, feeling relaxed, warm, and safe. Sit for a minute, enjoy the relaxation and comfort while practice your breathing.

Breathe in slowly through the nose, filling your lungs. Hold for a second, and then slowly exhale through the mouth. If it helps to create a rhythm, breathe in to the count of three and after holding for a second, breathe out to the count of three. The long and steady breaths fill you with the light and energy of the universe.

As you relax, sink further and further into the chair. With each breath you exhale, you feel yourself sinking deeper and deeper into the chair. Relax. Now picture how the floor feels on your feet. If the floor is carpeted experience the sensation of material against your feet; soft, warm and safe. If the floor is hardwood, experience the strength and coolness of the surface against your skin.

Ten. You sink further into the chair, and relax.

Nine.

Eight. Your body feels heavy, pulling you further into the chair.

Seven.

Six. Your arms and legs are now too heavy to move as you sink deeper into the chair.

Five.

Four. Deeper into the chair, you feel safe and fully relaxed.

Three.

Two. Deeper and deeper, you start to feel the cool forest floor beneath your feet.

One. Deeper and deeper, and relax.

You are seated on a small wooden bench. It is quite an old bench that has seen many visitors and feels well-worn. You sit still, thinking about all the people who have sat there before you, where they came from, and the energy they have left in the forest for you. It brings you comfort. Looking down at your body, you see that your clothes have been replaced with a simple cotton robe. The soft white material extends past your knees but allows for full movement. The robe is soft against your skin and as you lift the sleeve to your nose, the scent of fresh wild flowers fills your heart with joy. From your seated position you scan your immediate surroundings; the forest extends far past your vision yet it bodes a feeling of closeness and almost a coziness.

A simple path of soft wooden mulch winds away from you, splitting the forest in two. The large trees, though plentiful, don't project a sense of fullness as wide spaces provide a chance for ferns and wild flowers to grow. Signs of life fill your ears yet all you see are the bumblebees as they flutter from flower to flower, collecting pollen and fertilizing the next generation of flowers in your forest. Looking up towards the tall treetops, small patches of the blue sky reach through the canopy providing patches of golden sunlight on the forest floor breaking up the shade.

Looking down the path, you see glints of light as the sun reflects off the gentle flowing stream that crosses your path. The shallow sound of the life-bringing-water provides a rhythm for the forest as it passes over smooth river rocks. Looking beyond the stream, the bright light illuminating a natural treed archway suggests a sun-bathed clearing.

You sit content on the bench. Your toes dig in the wooden mulch of the path, discovering pockets of cool dampness as they explore below the surface. This is now your forest, your very own secret garden.

Closing your eyes, you breathe in the essence that is the forest. The cool fresh air fills your lungs as you relax and place your hands in your lap. The sounds of the forest fade as you continue to breathe.

In through your nose, out through your mouth; long steady breaths. The wooden bench feels softer, the sounds of the stream now just a whisper as you concentrate on your breathing.

Deep breaths; in through your nose, out through your mouth. The sounds of the forest fade away as your sense of the chair returns. You keep your eyes closed as your awareness returns; you feel the chair and the floor, and the cotton robes have been replaced with your own clothes.

One last steady breath; in through your nose, out through your mouth. Open your eyes.

Congratulations. You just took your first steps in creating your own safe place. Each time you visit your secret garden it will take on more of your energy and will become connected to you and your subconscious mind. You can do anything you like in your garden. Try planting your favorite flowers then upon your return, observe how they have grown. Are they vibrant and healthy or withered and sparse? Is there anything in your life that could be attributed to their progress?

The forest may remain as you leave it or you may find that a new path has revealed itself. The forest will respond according to your life and provide an intimate connection between your life and subconscious mind.

Sabbats

Imbolg/Imbolc ~ February 2nd

Ostara/Spring Equinox ~ March 20th

Beltane ~ April 30th

Midsummer/Litha/Summer Solstice ~ June 21st

Lughnasadh ~ August 1st

Mabon/Autumn Equinox ~ September 23rd

Samhain ~ October 31st

Yule/Winter Solstice ~ December 22nd

Ripples in the Pond

or the most part, I have led a solitary spiritual life. Of course there have been interactions along the way; chance meetings and fleeting friendships but in the end it was always my path to walk alone. This is not to be confused with the physical world around me where I shared many wonderful friendships and relationships. My spiritual journey was pretty much safe-guarded from the outside world. I don't think this was an intentional act on my part, it just happened that way.

One can be an extrovert in the physical world while the spiritual self might reflect an introverted shyness, providing a much-needed balance. I guess you could have considered me somewhat anti-social when it came to my spiritual journey and more so concerning matters of magic; be it black, white, or any other colour.

I found it easier to close people out, play the consummate comic for the world around me, and push my spiritual needs down somewhere between last night's Brussel sprouts and that trifle from last Christmas. It was not until I started exploration through paranormal investigations did I think about opening up to new spiritual paths and possibilities. I was urged, nay, convinced to develop my intuition and third-eye sight. Initially reluctant, my results progressed from seemingly lucky guesses to an unwavering knowing. Perhaps there was more out there for me beyond the tarnished path of a solitary pagan.

As the title of this chapter suggests, creating ripples is about just that. Taking a stone and throwing it into the furthest most reaches of your spiritual pond and allowing the ripples to carry forth opportunity and understanding. It's okay if you miss the first ripple, there will be another. Just as the ripples in a pond subside until they are immeasurable, the intensity of the message may also waver causing you to miss it completely. The number of stones you have to throw into the pond is entirely up to you. How many opportunities do you create for yourself? How many do you allow to lap against the bank before you decide to acknowledge and act upon them?

Let's take a recent opportunity that presented itself to me, and how this has affected my very own pond. One of my now best friends came into my life by random chance, or was it?

The initial contact had nothing really to do with me at all as Gordon was an old school friend of my girlfriend at the time. She was offering photography portraits at no charge as she honed her skill practicing on unsuspecting victims. So the pebble had been thrown into my pond and the ripples began to emanate from the epicenter of the impact. What was I to do?

Gordon had just finished his book and wanted a photo for the cover and Wendy was more than happy to oblige. As the time drew closer Wendy creeped his Facebook, as she often did, and relayed to me Gordon's achievements within the world of spiritual mediumship. Having missed the first ripple due to my own disconnect with the situation, this second ripple was brought to my attention with vigor.

The day arrived and passed. Gordon got his photo and life carried on. The ripples from the stone still created concentric rings of opportunity in my pond, though they had begun to weaken and barely made it to the edges.

It was not until months later as I planned an event at a local haunted bed and breakfast that I decided to contact Gordon, inviting him to attend or better still, to host a séance. Nothing. No replies, not even an acknowledgement on Facebook. Had the ripples run their course?

With the final attempt, I received a reply. To my surprise, he was very open to the séance and demonstrated great enthusiasm that led to many meetings prior to the event. It was during these meetings that we really started to connect as we had similar views and philosophies regarding the paranormal, spirituality, and everyday life.

I didn't know it at the time but by casting a stone in that spiritual pool, ripples were created that would change my life. The act of writing this book was one of the ripples from that stone, though it is just the latest in a long series of events that opened up doors within both my spiritual and physical life. I am now on a new path both physically and spirituality with many of these changes attributed to that first stone thrown by chance...or was it?

Throwing the stone is one thing; acknowledging and acting upon the resulting ripples is another. Some of us stand by the pool, never casting a stone, wondering why there is even a pool there in the first place. Others toss in a stone with little conviction. The shallow ripples barely ebb to the edge of the pond, dispersing long before reaching you. Some throw the stone as far as they can into the middle of the pond, producing strong ripples of opportunity that they welcome with openness and acceptance.

It is not always easy to accept change or accept that a change is necessary, but by doing so we take a step closer to obtaining our next stone. Will you gently lob in the stone and watch as the ripples of your opportunity wash away or will you throw the stone with conviction and embrace the subsequent ripples for the opportunities they create? Or maybe you will simply stand by the pond wondering why there is a pond in the first place.

Pay it Forward

Life is not always about you.
Sometimes you are simply there to allow others to live theirs.

LIVE LIFE FOR OTHERS AS YOU LIVE FOR YOURSELF

New Horizons

o, what will happen next on my madcap spiritual adventure?

As these items are from 2014, they are not so much New Horizons any longer but On Reflections. I have always had the propensity to look out for others and a recent project I undertook was no exception to this rule. My brother Ian passed when he was twenty-nine from an industrial accident. The machine he was working on had been missing the guards for quite some time despite a report being submitted to the health and safety department. An incident led to his passing but it is not something I openly talk about and don't care to elaborate on at this juncture.

I was talking to Gordon one day and recalling when I was informed of Ian's accident and how I had still not really grieved. I think with being so far removed physically, it was easier to detract myself from the reality of the given situation. The accident happened after I had been out of the country for five years and I suppose in my mind, everything was as I left it. If I bore no witness on a daily basis, the disconnect I felt became my reality. The whole situation was very confusing for me and if I stop long enough to really give it some thought, it still is.

Gordon is always trying to help me, even when I don't need it, but on this occasion I guess I did. He suggested that I write a letter to my brother then discard it in a fashion I deemed appropriate. The act of writing the letter to bring closure to things that I never got the chance to say is a technique used as part of the grieving process. Gordon has been a counsellor for many years so I always value his advice but it still took me a few days before I gave it further thought. Now anyone who knows me will attest to the fact that I rarely rest on my laurels and always look for a bigger and better way to do things. This was no exception.

The letters become a shining beacon of hope for others.

Instead of writing a letter I decided to create a website that would allow anyone write a letter to a lost loved one. *Dear Last Letter* is a virtual universe where each letter becomes a permanent star in the ever-expanding universe. Users of the site can add a story or simply read stories left by others and take inspiration or courage from their words.

I do plan to expand upon this initial idea through the addition of other avenues of expression.

I read about scrying pools and mirrors when I was an early teen, and even tried to make my own a few times using black dinner plates and water. Though my ability to concentrate for no more than a few minutes had always worked against me, I did manage some small successes. With the passing of my brother I really wanted to see if I could continue where

I had left off and even take it beyond simple scrying. In stepped Dr. Raymond Moody.

Inspired by his work and research, I plan to continue the studies into reunions with loved ones who have passed. If you are unfamiliar with the term psychomanteum, it is an ancient form of scrying once used by the ancient Greeks. The methods varied but often involved the use of a water-filled black reflecting bowl. The modern approach utilizes an angled mirror, a comfortable armchair, and a darkened room to create a similar environment. A single light source is placed behind the chair with the desired result being a visitation from a passed loved one.

I am not sure where this research will lead, but it an idea that has surfaced many times over the last decade. Not wanting to overlook another opportunity, I do plan to commence the research in early 2015.

A reading I received on a trip to Lily Dale revealed that I had always been a healer and teacher. For fifty lifetimes I had walked the same path, so I figure why fight it, let's go with it and see where it takes me. I remember one meditation session at my friend Sue's. Sue owned property where I used the ITC audio and captured what seemed to be alien-like sounds.

I was there with Pam for a visit when Sue offered to do a healing on me. Using her argon blanket and a number of crystals, she proceeded in leading the meditation and healing. I could hear both Sue and Pam as they proceeded to work the healing, but there were other voices, voices of people that should not have been in the room with us.

Upon waking from the meditation Sue suggested that there could be a connection to beings beyond this plane of existence. Also, three energies had been present from the great council. She had additionally received information on healing methodology and how my body interacted with the universe to supply healing energy. I know that this all sounds crazy, but it wasn't the first time I was told these types of things.

At Lily Dale I received another reading that was going swimmingly before the woman suddenly stopped what she was saying and looked up at me, stating I was not from this place. On another occasion, a psychic informed me that I was indeed a star-person or star-child. These psychics were not related in any way and the readings spanned over a three-year period.

With all that in mind it is no wonder I have been drawn to the healing arts. Having stumbled through distance healing using my very own 'wing it' method, I applied what came naturally but I think it was more luck than management.

In the interest of offering a more solid form of healing I decided to study reiki and have recently achieved my certification. During my first healing session that was part of the Reiki Level Two course I felt quite exposed and vulnerable. I knew I had to do a reading but I really hadn't put any thought into how I was going to achieve it. What I decided to do was take my new reiki knowledge and apply it to a healing I would normally have performed. This meant witchcraft.

I didn't have my herbs with me so I used what was there. The same could be said for my oils, but we made do.

The first thing I did was balance my chakras then applied a synchronicity to the young woman receiving reiki. The session continued and what was expected to take thirty minutes lasted almost an hour. I had no candles so I used mental images of certain candles to apply a focused point of energy where it was needed. It felt great to mix reiki with witchcraft and my 'wing it' method. It's not exactly a pure form of the art but it's my form.

The Scole experiment holds a fascination that has stayed with me ever since we organized a lecture on the subject for the paranormal group ten years ago. The president of the Scottish Paranormal Society was kind enough to offer us an insight into the amazing discoveries the experiment uncovered during those years in a dark cramped village basement in Scole, England. The act of physical mediumship harkens back to the golden years of psychic phenomenon when almost anything seemed possible and dare I say it, plausible. Things have changed over the years. We now find ourselves dealing with a very cynical world where we question everything and accept only what we can see or touch.

I have taken the first steps into our very own experiments and will be conducting bi-weekly sessions with Gordon and guests as soon as we can get the room ready. I am thinking of setting up a Scole-cam for live footage. This cam will be free to observe and afford anyone with an internet connection the opportunity to observe a session from anywhere in the world.

I know you are all interested in what will happen to my three paranormal groups now that I am a well-known author. Worry not, I have big plans for the groups and will be exploring the return of the Gathering for its third iteration. The Gathering is a full day event that culminates at midnight at the conclusion of the last séance. A single entry fee secures up to four psychic readings, meditation circles, séances, psychomanteum use and advice, workshops, lecture, gallery readings, healings, food, vendors, and of course, time spent with yours truly.

In terms of investigations, there has been a downward shift from investigations that cross the U.S. border. This may be related to the requirement to hold a passport or just the additional travel costs; either way, I will be concentrating more on locations within Canada for the foreseeable future.

Will there be any other books now I have managed to actually finish this one?

Well, this first book has really given me the impetus to explore future publications. I have a number of books in mind with the next one dedicated to healing and how I merged Reiki with Witchcraft. This second title will be a working volume with easy to follow examples and guides to how you can evolve your healing potential across opposing models. Look for this title in 2015.

In closing I would like to reiterate an important theme to your spiritual journey. Please remember that this is YOUR journey, you are not on this path for anyone but yourself. Others may benefit from your growth but that should only be a bi-product not your goal. If you decide to participate in a paranormal investigation, don't get hung up on proving anything to anyone but yourself. If they need to understand and accept then their own journey will lead them to that place, if not then they are just not ready. Just as you are the center of your own journey, so they are to theirs. Respect their journey and subsequent choices, after all that could have been you at one time.

As for me, my own journey continues. Where it leads is a story I have yet to write. The one thing I am now certain of, no matter what my choices in life are, they will all be my own, they will all be spiritual, and they will most definitely be madcap.

Glossary

Candle Magic: One of the simplest forms of spell casting with the colours representing various aspects of life and our spiritual path.

Chakras: Part of the subtle body, not the physical body, and as such are the meeting points of the subtle (non-physical) energy channels called nadiis. Western tradition associates colours with each chakra. The seven main chakras are, Root (Red), Sacral (Orange), Solar Plexus (Yellow), Heart (Green), Throat (Light Blue), Third Eye (Dark Blue), Crown (Violet or White).

DVR: (Digital Video Recorder) An electronics device or application software that records video in a digital format to a disk drive.

EVP: (Electronic voice phenomena) Sounds found on electronic recordings which resemble speech.

Incense – (stick, cone, powder): Aromatic biotic material which releases fragrant smoke when burned.

K2 Meter: A device made in the United States that monitors Electromagnetic Fields (EMF) and displays any changes through a series of LEDs.

Lily Dale: A spiritualist community of the Modern Spiritualist movement located in Chautauqua County, New York, USA.

Meditation: A practice in which an individual trains the mind or induces a mode of consciousness.

Mediums: See Mediumship.

Mediumship: The practice of certain people—known as mediums—to purportedly mediate communication between spirits of the dead and the living.

Mirrors: Can be used as a portal by ghosts and other entities allowing them pass from their realm into the one of the living. This has never been proven and remains a theory or folktale.

Oils (Essential): Concentrated aromatic liquids derived from plants and often used in magic and aromatherapy.

Orbs: On occasion have been interpreted as spirit phenomena within the paranormal community. These artifacts can show signs of intelligence and self-illumination.

Ouija board: Also known as a spirit or talking board has been utilized in some guise for thousands of years. The modern Ouija is a flat board containing the letters of the alphabets, numbers, "yes," "no" and often includes a "good bye."

Psychic readings: An attempt to discern information through the use of heightened perceptive abilities and/or a connection with a spirit guide(s) or celestial being.

Readings: See Psychic Readings

Scole experiments: Were a series of mediumistic séances held in a small British town in the Nineties. Practicing physical mediumship these experiments claim to provide proof of spirit energies.

Scrying: The practice of looking into a ball (typically crystal) or a reflective surface with the belief that spiritual information or visions can be achieved. It can also be used for divination or fortune-telling purposes.

Séance: An attempt to communicate with spirits while traditionally seated at a table with two or more participants. One of the earliest books on the subject was published in 1760 with a dramatic increase in popularity during the mid-eighteen century.

Shadow people: The belief that a patch of shadow is a spiritual figure and often considered a malevolent entity.

Spirit guides: A term for an entity that remains a disincarnate spirit in order to act as a guide or protector to a living person.

Star children: Believed to have been sent here from places in the universe. They possess psychic, spiritual, and other extra-sensory abilities.

Tarot cards: Possess pictures and titles that represent a specific concept. The belief in divination associated with Tarot focuses on the prospect that whatever cards are dealt to the participant will be revelatory.

UFOs: Unidentified Flying Object. The Oxford English Dictionary refers to a UFO as "An unidentified flying object; a 'flying saucer'."

References

Books

King, Stephen, *The Stand,* Bantam, Doubleday, Dell, 1978.

McLindon, Byrne, Goldenfein, Heriot, *The Secret*, Prime Time Publications, 2006.

Redfield, James, *The Celestine Prophecy,* Warner Books Inc., 1993.

Redfield, James, *The Tenth Insight,* Warner Books Inc., 1996.

Wattles, Wallace, *The Science of Getting Rich,* The Elizabeth Towne Company of Holyoke, MA, USA., 1910.

Movies and TV Shows

Apollo 13, directed by Ron Howard, Warner Bros., 1995.

Contact, directed by Robert Zemeckis, Warner Bros., 1997.

Fastwalkers, directed by Anthony T. Miles, Anderson Digital, 2006.

True Blood, Your Face Goes Here Entertainment, 2008.

Websites

Spirituality, Paranormal 101,
www.meetup.com/SpiritualityParanormal101Niagara/
Paranormal 101 – Facebook, www.facebook.com/PIST101

Dear Last Letter. www.dearlastletter.com

The Scole Experiment. www.thescoleexperiment.com